Mike has captured the essence of both the heartaches and the high points of a profession that is incredibly rewarding.
Dan Kleman, ICMA President, 1993

Managing cities and counties is not a science; it is a mixture of ethics, art and experience. These stories help us immensely by conveying values, experience and even myths which not only allow us to reflect on our own successes, failures and foibles but to learn from our fellows who are also trying to make Democracy work.
Norm King, ICMA President, 1995

A local government manager's life is a journey that includes incredible experiences that are more than mere stories – they are lessons, and these stories are lessons to be shared for those continuing in the profession.
Dave Mora, ICMA President, 2001

Stories represent the original way we all learned. They educate and communicate the great lessons in life in a way that is personal, yet applicable for all. Mike, thanks for putting together the best of the best of life lessons!
Peggy Merriss, ICMA President, 2002

The compassion and wisdom of Mike Conduff is evidenced on a daily basis to his friends and strangers alike. His personal touch on stories from his public service peers comes from his heart directly into the heart of the reader.
Dave Krings, ICMA President, 2003

Mike has captured the very essence of local government – making people's lives work better through community building. The stories he relates provide an inspiration for us all.
Ed Daley, ICMA President 2007

Experience is the ultimate teacher. If we are wise we learn not only from our own actions but the experience of others. The practical advice from these stories will be helpful to those of us who are long in this local government profession, and invaluable to those who are new to it.

Tom Lundy, ICMA President, 2004

This wonderful collection of tales from professional local government managers is about the getting of wisdom from those that have been there. Through its wonderful stories, thoughtful insights and great quotes, it is the power of story-telling of life on the frontline at its best. Read, laugh, learn!

Michael Willis, ICMA President, 2005

John Adams said that people and nations are formed by the fires of adversity. Mike has captured how the Green Berets of local government management overcome adversity and lead communities to successful outcomes in complex times. They are experts at blending efficiency and results with ethics and involvement.

David Limardi, ICMA President, 2008

The next best thing to personal experience is learning from others in similar circumstances. *Democracy at the Doorstep* showcases those who have "been there and done that!"

Jim Starr, TCMA President, 1992

As a former President of TCMA I am honored to be a part of this great profession. As I enter into retirement, I cherish all the thoughts, memories and friendships that membership in TCMA has provided me. *Democracy at the Doorstep* is a great collection of those. Remember – if you don't know where you are going you'll never know when you get there.

Gordon Pierce, TCMA President, 1993

The stories in *Democracy at the Doorstep* are a home run! Well done, Mike!

Jim Blagg, TCMA President, 1990

Story-telling is a simple, but invaluable tool for managers in providing leadership, changing organizational culture, and conveying organizational objectives. Mike's book is full of useful stories that can serve these practical purposes.

James Thurmond, TCMA President, 1995

In *Democracy at the Doorstep* Mike has taken real-life city management stories and applied lessons for us all to benefit from – no matter our experience or background. Thanks Mike for a job well done!

Ron Cox, TCMA President, 1997

It is so true that city management professionals see and deal with some very, very interesting situations. Mike's compilation of these experiences into stories and application of lessons learned are not only a treat to read but meaningful as well.

Melissa Byrne Vossmer, TCMA President, 1999

If you have ever heard Mike speak, you know he has a gift for storytelling. In this collection, each story has a lesson to be learned. And it is not just about city government; each can be applied in your own personal and professional life. Mike's use of humor makes his lessons enjoyable and fun. Relax, read, enjoy, and learn.

Nick Finan, TCMA President, 2000

Mike has done a great job of capturing some of the best stories of City Managers who are "in the trenches." I know you will enjoy hearing from professionals whose experiences will inspire, motivate and instruct.

Larry Gilley, TCMA President, 2003

Democracy at the Doorstep is hilarious, but true....Mike you hit it long and straight with these experiences; thanks for sharing!

Craig Lonon, TCMA President, 2004

I try to live by the adage, "During any given week something will occur I never thought possible!" and Mike's stories prove that is true!

Rickey Childers, TCMA President, 2005

Democracy at the Doorstep provides a peek into the reality of what managing a city is like from the inside. I highly recommend it to anyone interested in local government and especially to all young professionals who are thinking about a rewarding career in this great field.

Mark McDaniel, TCMA President, 2006

One of the best ways to learn is from stories that teach leadership and management principles. Great job, Mike!

Mike Perez, TCMA President, 2007

Mike, great stories; I wish I had read them earlier in my career – I wouldn't have made so many mistakes!

Paul Parker, TCMA President, 2008

Mike has captured the message that City Managers – and those who love them – want and need to hear. *Democracy at the Doorstep* speaks the language of Managers and I applaud Mike's efforts to capture the 'war stories' of our profession.

Courtney Sharp, TCMA President 2009

Great stories are great learning tools. Mike has brought together a wealth of public manager stories with valuable lessons for any manager.

Brad Mears, KACM President, 2002

Democracy at the Doorstep's stories from city managers in the trenches are great learning opportunities. A fun read and full of valuable lessons.

John Deardoff, KACM President, 2003

Reading Mike's work had been inspiring. His experience in our profession has given him a unique place to compile and report our stories. These will cause us to look back at what we have done and put ourselves in the pages of this book. This will be another of those standing stones in the history of our profession.

Larry Paine, KACM President, 2006

Mike is committed to capturing our profession's history of service through story telling. With *Democracy at the Doorstep* he sends you back in time where you can feel the excitement of opportunity and conflict of competing values in a way those who serve the public will appreciate.

Matt Allen, KACM President, 2009

In this exciting new book, *Democracy at the Doorstep – True Stories from the Green Berets of Public Administrators*, Mike Conduff has captured the essence of what it takes to be a City Manager. The insights shared reflect not only the values of the profession, but Mike's long and steadfast commitment to excellence in public service. He has been both a mentor and inspiration to me in my career in city management. Every time I hear Mike speak or read his words in print, I am reminded that it is a privilege to have the opportunity to serve, and to be in a position to make a difference.

Cathy Holdeman, KACM President, 2010

Thanks for the well-written stories that we all can relate to and learn from! Exceptional job Mike!

Randy Partington, KACM President, 2011

I love the stories! I remember one about Mike and me crawling through a dense, thorny mesquite thicket on a gulf coast golf course to retrieve an errant driver our golf team partner threw deep. Of course I can't tell it yet – that will have to go in the next book!

Ron Bowman, TPPA President, 2004

Mike has always had the gift of teaching through story telling. You will love these learnings and be inspired by the stories. Democracy works, and *Democracy at the Doorstep* is a testimonial to part of the reason why!

Stan Stewart, KACM President, 1990

As President of ICMA I was always impressed with the caliber of professionals who give so much to make Democracy work. Like all elite Special Forces members these folks have great stories to tell. Mike has captured so many of those here in *Democracy at the Doorstep,* and if you have any interest at all in local government you will find this a must read. By the way – the Learnings are Universal.

Bill Buchanan, ICMA President, 2006

In my 42 years in public administration I have heard and seen and told a lot of helpful stories from the world of local government. It is great to have *Democracy at the Doorstep* as a compilation of these types of experiences to enable some of us to reflect on the past, and others of us to learn for the future!

Karl Nollenberger, ICMA President, 1994

The road is long and dusty in the City Management business – but when we look back on our careers, there are many bright spots like the ones Mike shares in *Democracy at the Doorstep*. Thanks, Mike!

Lou Fox, TCMA President, 1986

Democracy
at the
Doorstep

True Stories and Key Insights
from the "Green Berets"
of Public Administrators

Contents

Foreword

The premise of *Democracy at the Doorstep – True Stories from the Green Berets of Public Administrators* is a sound one. The Founding Fathers knew that government closest to the people was best and it is at the local level that the majority of individuals experience government, and democracy. Think of it this way; most people who deal with a court system deal with a municipal or county court. Most who need emergency assistance receive it from local police, fire and EMS professionals. Those who enjoy safe drinking water and sanitary sewer facilities receive those services from local government. Most people who utilize public facilities (parks, playgrounds, ball fields, recreation centers, swimming pools, etc.) utilize municipal facilities. When you reflect on it, most of our experiences with government are with local government, and in most of those local governments there is a professional staff person – a city or county manager – that makes sure things work properly.

What Mike Conduff does is put a face on these men and women for us. By sharing their stories he shows us what they believe in and care about and sacrifice for. Duty for a city or county manager, much like duty for a Green Beret is paramount. Sworn to uphold the Charter of the community they serve these professionals regularly put citizens ahead of themselves and on occasion ahead of even their own families. Money cannot and does not buy that kind of loyalty; only commitment does.

I learned my lessons about commitment during my undergraduate days at the University of Kansas in the early sixties where I was a member of the US Army ROTC Program during an interesting time in the history of the country. Upon graduation I was commissioned as a second lieutenant and the Army sent me directly to Fort Bragg, North Carolina to join a military intelligence unit in support of the 82nd Airborne Division. After spending over a year there and learning great life skills like how to be a prisoner of war interrogator and to jump out of airplanes, I was sent to the Panama Canal Zone to a military intelligence detachment supporting the 8th Special Forces Group. I was honored to wear the Green Beret as part of this unit. (The fact that I did, as you will read later, is totally coincidental to the title of this book!)

While in Panama, I spent much of my time as an instructor at the Army's Jungle Operations Course. This was an incredibly rigorous course designed to prepare its participants with knowledge about how to exist and operate and survive in a jungle environment. Nearly all of our graduates went directly from the Canal Zone to combat in Viet Nam.

Upon reflection, spending as much time as I did in this real jungle, learning to deal with unexpected hazards, and maintaining a sense of direction while in the midst of a very tangled, messy environment, was undoubtedly good preparation for a career in city management!

After leaving the Army I returned to the University of Kansas for graduate school. I did my MPA program internship with Bob Kipp who was then City Manager in Fairborn, OH. Bob has been an outstanding mentor, friend, and role model for me ever since that time. I had the opportunity to work with Bob a second time in Kansas City, MO. He was by that time City Manager there and asked me to join him as an Assistant City Manager.

Spending four years working with Bob in Kansas City was an extremely valuable learning experience. At the same time it was not always easy. During these four years, Kansas City was engaged in a protracted battle with the Firefighters Union which culminated in a four-day strike. Following the strike, my job was to be the city's representative in the negotiation of a new agreement with the Union. To describe these negotiations as tense and difficult would be a gross understatement. They also at times became very personal. In fact, on one occasion the Union decided to picket our home. So for a few days we had firefighters outside our home strolling around our cul-de-sac with picket signs. Our children, who were quite small, suggested that they should set up a lemonade stand and make a little money. (The classic case of making lemonade when life hands you lemons!)

It was during this time that I became even more active in our professional association, the International City/County Management Association. One of the nice things about service in ICMA is the opportunity to meet talented and committed individuals. Indeed, I first met Mike Conduff a number of years ago while serving on the Board of the ICMA. He was already an active member and we became even more acquainted when he came to Bryan, Texas in 1992. He has been a great friend since that time. He was kind enough to introduce me to Dr. John Carver and the Policy Governance® Model. Mike's book based on Policy Governance®, *The OnTarget Board Member – 8 Indisputable Behaviors*, should be required reading for all newly elected officials.

After Mike moved to Denton we have been able to visit on an even more frequent basis and it is always fun to find out about the latest greatest trends in local government when we are together. Mike's network is an international one and he always seems to know who is doing what where. In his role as Senior Advisor for Governance for ICMA he helps cities all across the country.

I am especially honored to be a part of this endeavor. Mike is one of those rare individuals who combines possessing a strong intellectual curiosity and exploration with delivering equally strong practical results. He has demonstrated this capability during his days in city management and now as a consultant and author. This book epitomizes this exceptional combination by using everyday practical stories from the lives of city managers which, when studied, produce key insights, lessons and learning opportunities for all of us with an interest in urban management. I shall always treasure the favorite saying of Dr. Edwin O. Stene who founded the KU City Management Training Program: "Experience is your best teacher – provided you study your lessons." We all have an opportunity to study the lessons contained in this important book.

Even though *Democracy at the Doorstep – True Stories from the Green Berets of Public Administrators* is an easy book to read, I encourage you to digest it slowly. Ponder the True Stories and the Key Insights. Think about the quotes. It is my hope that when you are done you will have a greater appreciation for these "Green Berets," these men and women in the cities and towns of our great country that truly Keep Democracy Strong.

Bob Herchert
Fort Worth, Texas, USA

Inspiration for the Title

After 30 years in local government, the last 25 of those spent as a City Manager in four different university communities, I have a great and enduring admiration for the men and women who serve the public in the towns, cities and counties of our great country. As citizens we often look to the Whitehouse or the State Capitol for public policy decisions of import. But the fact is that what happens every day of the year in City Halls and County Courthouses across America impacts us the most.

While I very much appreciate the U.S. Armed Forces – having grown up in a career Air Force Officer's family, and particularly in this anxious time internationally – and while I largely understand the need for federal and state agencies, it is the services that I get from my local community that influence my quality of life the most. And this is true for most of us.

When we call 911, we have a public safety response from incredible professionals in minutes. When we get in our cars, we drive on efficient and safe street systems with traffic control devices that function. When we flip our electric switches, lights come on. When we turn the tap, water is there. When we flush, it goes away. Our fees or taxes for this are very reasonable, especially in contrast to the Federal Income Tax we pay. In fact the tax tab for most local schools to operate is multiples of the local government's.

From an access perspective, if you want to talk to the

President or Governor you had best be a big contributor or a brother-in-law. If you have a complaint with a large utility, retailer or other provider of service and want to talk to the president of the company or chairman of the board you had better own a lot of shares of stock. However, if you want to talk to the Mayor or City Manager, just pick up the phone!

Largely because of this access and the accompanying accountability, it is at the local level that Democracy truly thrives.

The Congress and most state legislatures exempt themselves from regulations they promulgate on local governments. While legislatures routinely close their doors and do deals behind them, open meetings are commonplace in your community and you are most welcome to attend. Want a copy of about anything that exists there? Just ask. Want to get involved? Just volunteer – you will be welcomed with open arms.

As a City Manager and now long-time governance consultant, I have met and worked with many tremendous elected officials all across the country. These are folks who give hugely of their time and energy for no more reward than seeing their community improve and prosper. They are rarely paid, rarely thanked, and often maligned. There is no retirement program after their terms, and they don't get pensions or health insurance.

When you think about it you have to wonder why anyone would even want a job like that.

These elected officials work hard to understand the will of the people and harder to bring it to fruition. Even the ones I haven't agreed with or liked very well I have admired. Putting your name on a ballot takes a lot of courage. Going door-to-door to get elected is not for the faint of heart.

While I routinely sing the praises of local elected officials, I believe it is the Professional Managers and Administrators in Cities and Counties that are really on the front lines of Democracy. It is one of the true "24/7" positions. Their every moment is subject to the call of duty to their communities. They are the unsung heroes that keep Democracy strong.

Some twenty-five years ago I attended an ICMA Mountain Plains Regional Meeting in Colorado organized by that incredible professional, ICMA Director of Member Services, Betsy Sherman. Ken Torp, a professor in Boulder and the seminar leader expressed his admiration for the profession by saying, "City and County Managers are the Green Berets of Public Administrators." The metaphor stuck with me all these years. Of course he was right, and in the course of implementing the policy of the councils they serve, these Special Forces professionals have seen and experienced remarkable triumphs and stunning disasters.

While serving as President of the Texas Association of City Management I had the opportunity to travel our great state and meet or reconnect with hundreds of these professionals. Wherever they gather they tell the tales of their encounters with Democracy. These are their true stories and their key insights.

Acknowledgements

Three renowned City Managers have been heroes of mine as I have faced my own challenges to foster Democracy. As a probably too young City Manager (just 27!) in Pittsburg, Kansas I walked into one of my first statewide annual Kansas Association of City/County Management meetings in the Manhattan, Kansas Holidome knowing virtually no one in the room. Buford Watson, the always effervescent City Manager of Lawrence looked up, realized he didn't know me and came straight over to introduce himself. He took hold of my arm and didn't let go; including me in his circles for the rest of his too short life. Buford's smile, laugh and professionalism were a model to me and to many others. The Buford Watson Award given by the Kansas Association of City/County Management is an enduring testimony to his legacy. Democracy took Buford from us early, but he was its most ardent supporter.

Bob Herchert, the former City Manager of Fort Worth, Texas, and now Chairman of the Board of Freese and Nichols, an internationally recognized engineering company, and Baldridge Award winner is cut from the same cloth as Buford. In the celebratory moments, Bob is always ready to share the triumphs. And in the dark times that all soldiers on the front lines face, Bob is just as faithful. A note, a card, an e-mail, a phone call or a lunch with Bob is guaranteed to lift your spirits. His advice is sound and his character is rock solid.

Bob also adds to the inspiration for the subtitle for this book. In his early days Bob actually was a Green Beret. Training to parachute behind enemy lines served as an excellent precursor to the council meetings and public hearings he survived in his career!

Tom Muehlenbeck, the acclaimed City Manager of Plano completes my trio. I have known Tom since the late 1980's when we both served on the ICMA Public Policy Committee, and long before I came to Texas. Besides his unremitting professionalism and dedication, Tom personally altered the course of my management career when he unselfishly got on an airplane and flew to Bryan, Texas one evening to provide a testimonial for John Carver's Policy Governance® model to our City Council.

Some of the council members were really gung ho about Policy Governance, but I wasn't so sure. Although the model "sounded good" it was Tom's endorsement that ultimately tipped the scales for me, and I have never looked at local government governance in quite the same way since.

Being able to work closely with Tom on the Board of the Texas City Management Association and at ICMA where we both served as Regional Vice-Presidents has been a real treat.

Of course, since this is a book of many managers' stories I would certainly be remiss if I did not give due credit to this profession and the outstanding men and women who serve in it. I have been exceedingly privileged to serve as President of both the Kansas and Texas City/County Management Associations, and on the Board of the International City/County Management Association. In the course of those labors of love I have been blessed to meet almost all of my very best friends. Whether it is from serving in big cities or small towns or rural or urban counties, their stories bring their passion to make Democracy work to life.

Thanks to all of you who have influenced my life so

powerfully, and an especial thanks to those of you who have shared your stories with me!

Author's Personal Note

A work of this nature owes many debts. First of course, the inspiration for the book goes to my many incredible colleagues on the front lines of Democracy in the towns, cities, villages and counties across this great country, and beyond. Thanks folks for what you do every day to keep Democracy strong!

When Bill Buchanan (long tenured County Manager, Sedgwick County, Kansas) was President of ICMA he heard me give a talk about Democracy on the Doorstep and shared with me that he too used a similar theme. He generously gave of his ideas and beliefs, and in total abundance thinking gifted me full permission to use not only the title, but the ideas. Bill has been a great friend and supporter over the years and was an exceptionally fine President for IMCA. Thanks Bill!

Betsy Sherman, Director of Member Services at ICMA, has coordinated a Mountain Plains Regional Meeting for City/County Managers in the states of Arkansas, Colorado, Idaho, Kansas, Montana, Nebraska, New Mexico, North Dakota, Oklahoma, South Dakota, Texas, Utah and Wyoming for many, many years. Although time has blurred the exactness of the memory I believe I first met Betsy in the Fall of 1983. She was as impressive then as now, and these conferences provided many key life moments for me. The subtitle for this book comes from one of those, and the fact that I came to Texas at all was a result of a conversation with John Harrison, then City Manager in Waco, TX, in Salt Lake City at one of Betsy's conferences. Betsy, you are leaving such an awesome legacy through your work!

I cannot start listing all of the folks in local government

that I have an obligation to. The list would be too long, and the fact is I would likely forget someone and later feel badly about leaving them out. However, a couple must be mentioned.

Terrell Blodgett, former City Manager and long time professor at the LBJ School in Austin is one of those. Already an icon in my early years, Terrell took me and my best buddy Stan Stewart under his wing in the mid-eighties and shared his love of local government along with advice and counsel. Terrell also nominated me for membership in the prestigious National Academy of Public Administration later in my career, where I have had the opportunity to rub elbows with and absorb knowledge from so many of the truly great public administrators of our times. Terrell, your writing is unsurpassed in our sphere. Many thanks!

Ernie Mosher was the Executive Director of the Kansas League of Municipalities when I got my first manager's job at age 27. I was what we would now call an "unconscious incompetent." (I was so dumb I didn't know that I didn't know.) Ernie helped me transition to the next stage—that of being a conscious incompetent. (I was still dumb, but at least I knew that I didn't know!)

Ernie dispensed his best advice late at night around a poker table. He had only one arm and it was a mesmerizing event to watch him smoke unfiltered cigarettes, drink straight Jack Daniels whiskey, shuffle, deal, bet and win with just his left hand. At 28 or 29 years of age I got my second masters degree at Ernie's poker table losing money to such greats as Virgil Basgall, Dean Wiley, George Pyle, and Don Harmon. They honored me by letting me bask in their light. I think I paid about as much in lost bets for their degree as I did in tuition for my MBA and have probably used their wisdom more.

These pioneers have all passed now, and somewhere along the way I have gone from being the young turk, forever tilting at windmills and asking "why," to being the establishment guy. As the Senior Advisor for Governance for ICMA [isn't that a horrible title? Couldn't it be, "younger than he looks" advisor, or, "not old, just wise" advisor?] I am honored to travel to many locations and it is so intriguing to me to be the person that folks look to for the history. My age cohort will pass next, but that is as it should be. The young turks are still there, keeping Democracy strong. My thanks to you for taking the difficult mantle of local government leadership on your shoulders!

On a personal level, my incredible wife, Kathy, and the young children God has gifted us with, Rebekah, Joseph and Jordan also get major thanks for allowing me the office time to capture these stories and present them properly. Writing is to some large degree a solitary task, and balancing time between the knocks on the office door, the hugs delivered therewith and the deadlines of publishing was always delicate. I hope the ratio was somewhere close to where it should have been. I love you all!

To the folks at RJ Communications, especially Jonathan Gullery, thanks for your continued support, customer service and timeliness. You have taught me much, guided me well and you have my published appreciation!

Prologue

As a very young City Manager I needed all the help I could get. The departing City Manager had treated me exceedingly well as an employee and assistant director and had even promoted me to a department head at age 25. He had given me opportunities to learn and to grow, and now I was going to sit in his chair. Although we had had our differences along the way I felt very obliged to him and was at least wise enough to ask for his advice as we wrapped up a three day transition process.

In response to my inquiry he simply told me this story.

The Three Envelopes

The lightning from the storm outside flashed brightly in the darkened room as the rain drummed on the windows of the second floor office. Deep in the throes of his dilemma, Jim was only dimly aware of the fury of the storm, but the sharp impact of the crashing thunder brought him immediately back to the present. Eyes straining, Jim stared at the three envelopes resting heavily in his hands. They had long been locked in his desk drawer, waiting for such a night as this one. His heart beat heavily as his fingers traced their linen texture. Written with a bold hand on each was a single large Roman numeral: I, II, III.

He thought back to the triumph of that first day in the office, not really so long ago. "City Manager" the doorplate read. "Successful" his wife said. The youngest to ever hold the position in this town. The paper with the front-page article. Even the family photo sitting on the shiny wooden desk. Yes, a great day.

His remembered his predecessor had stopped by to wish him well. Jim was polite, after all the older gentleman had been in the business quite a while. Too long, really, when you thought about it. Times had changed. An educated and professionally trained manager was what the town needed now. Nonetheless Jim felt the need to be polite. Although as the city manager he was really now too busy, he took time to thank the man for the peaceful and supportive transition.

Innocently, Jim had asked the older manager if he had any advice. (Just being nice.) That was when the three envelopes had appeared. "Here, put these in your desk. They contain the sum of what I have learned in my career. When you are faced with a crisis you can't seem to resolve, open one. But use them sparingly; when they are gone you will be too!"

Jim had chuckled then. A crisis? Those were things that happened to others. He was professionally trained. With good planning and his guidance there would be no crisis. In order to humor his guest he had made a great show of placing the envelopes in the upper right hand drawer. Promptly forgotten, there they had stayed. Until tonight.

He stared at the envelopes. How had it come to this? Was his job really in jeopardy? What would he tell his wife?

Slowly he opened envelope one. In it was a single sheet of paper with a single phrase written on it.

"Blame your predecessor."

Although he didn't really like doing it, Jim immediately knew it would work and sure enough it did. Enough time had passed that no one felt called upon to truly defend the former manager and enough folks bought into the excuse that Jim was able to survive. After awhile he even believed it. After all, it was his predecessor's fault.

Then, some time later, on another stormy night – this time a regular blizzard – Jim faced his second potential vote of no confidence. He had talked to the Mayor and to the Chair of the Chamber and even to the President of the University in the community and it still looked like he needed a miracle. He remembered how well the first envelope had turned out and rummaged in the desk until he found envelope two.

Although he hated to utilize this now rapidly dwindling resource Jim did not see another alternative. Again, haltingly he opened the envelope. In it was a single sheet of paper with a single word.

"Reorganize."

"Of course," Jim thought, "that will take the wind out of people's sails. They will see that I am a take charge guy and it will buy me the reprieve I need to solve the crisis."

After pulling an all nighter with the department heads Jim called a news conference and announced a major staff shakeup and reorganization. With the media trying to understand the new structure and council working with new staff contacts the crisis did indeed get resolved (well, sort of) and Jim survived once again.

However as even more time passed it ultimately became clear Jim was finished. As the Editor of the Local Newspaper had said just recently, "You can stick a fork in him, he's done!"

Jim could see no way out. It was far past time to try to blame his predecessor, and no way was a reorg going to work this time. He needed envelope three.

Having seen this day coming, Jim had placed the envelope, now somewhat yellow with age, on the corner of the desk. There it had waited, its siren song of another latent miracle calling to him. "At least it is not raining or snowing this time," he thought.

Hands shaking he opened the last envelope. Like the others there was a single sheet of paper. Written on that piece of paper were these few words:

"Prepare three envelopes for your successor."

After a few moments of listening to my obligatory chuckles my predecessor looked me in the eye and said, "Remember this. City Managers are Reformers. You were hired to do the right thing, irrespective of the cost. Consequently, in this business there are only two kinds of managers; those that have been let go, and those that will be."

The New Truck
(As told by Larry Fields)

Handling disgruntled citizens is a part of being the easily accessible CEO of a city. When people are really upset they want to see the top person. The ability to listen calmly to tirades without showing a lot of emotion is one of the hallmarks of successful city managers.

With that said, I clearly recall one such incident where my emotions got the better of me.

"There is a citizen out here who is demanding to speak to the City Manager," said my secretary. "He says we owe him a new truck."

Figuring this to be a traffic accident, a bad pothole or some such event I agreed to see the man.

After pretty curt introductions, his opening line was, "You owe me a new truck."

I asked why he thought the city should owe him a new truck.

"I have a lot of trees at my home, and I spent the weekend raking up leaves and burning them at the back by the alley," he said.

I nodded to show I was listening; all the while wondering how raking leaves could lead to the city needing to buy the gentleman a new truck.

"This morning I gathered the remains of all of the burned leaves and put them in my pickup to take to the landfill."

Again I nodded to let him know I was listening attentively.

"I got out there and they had me back down the slope towards the working face so I could dump them out on the pile."

Another nod, still wondering where this story was going.

"I shut the truck off and climbed out to empty it."

My neck was getting tired from the bobbing, but again I nodded.

"As I opened the tailgate I quickly discovered the wind created by the trip to the landfill had stirred up the embers. The open tailgate acted like a funnel for the wind, and the next thing I knew the back of my truck was on fire!"

At this point in the story I couldn't help but smile a little at the mental picture of a truck on the slope of the landfill on fire. Unfortunately the citizen noticed the small smile and began to raise his voice.

He went on, a bit louder. "I decided that if I jumped in the truck and accelerated up the hill, all of the burning remains would fall out."

That sounded reasonable. In fact I probably would have thought about doing the same thing, so again I nodded.

"I couldn't start the truck!"

This time while nodding I coughed a bit so I could use my hand to cover another involuntary smile.

"Since I couldn't start the truck I jumped out and ran up to the top of the hill and got your dozer operator. I shouted out my predicament to him and he quickly backed down to my truck and hooked a chain on the front."

Again I nodded, this time thinking, "Wow, that is a great response by the operator."

The citizen continued, "We were in such a hurry because of the fire that I forgot to take the truck out of gear, and when he let out the clutch on that big dozer, he pulled the front end off of the truck."

When this mental image flashed through my mind I felt my control slipping and a chuckle just slipped out.

The citizen was really annoyed at my laughing at his predicament, but the thought of the big Caterpillar Tractor pulling the bumper off of a pickup truck with a fire in its bed was getting the best of me.

Again covering my mouth and clearing my throat I nodded for him to go on.

"Since we couldn't move the truck I asked the operator to try smothering it by dumping a load of dirt in the bed."

My admiration for the citizen's resourcefulness kept going up. "Great idea," I complimented, and again nodded for him to continue.

"He picked up a big load of dirt and plopped it in the bed."

I nodded.

"The bucket on the dozer was so big that all of that dirt landing in the back of the truck overloaded the springs and tires and the whole back end collapsed."

This mental picture was more than I could bear, and I began to laugh uncontrollably. The more I tried to stop the more I laughed. I just kept seeing his truck sitting on the axles, with no front end, covered under several cubic yards of dirt.

Evidently the laughter was contagious because before long the citizen was joining me. We laughed so hard that we both had tears in our eyes.

Pretty soon the secretary came in to see what was going on and after telling her the story in abbreviated form she joined in the laughter. Before long the whole building was repeating the story.

In fact, every time I thought about it I laughed. Right up to the time that we wrote him a check for his new truck.

KEY INSIGHT

Empathetic listening is a great skill, and one that must be cultivated in the Manager's office. Often, just giving a citizen the opportunity to be heard and understood is all the remedy that is required. Add the ability to laugh and a sense of humor that can be used at the appropriate time and you have the ingredients for successful customer service.

"Listening is a magnetic and strange thing, a creative force. The friends who listen to us are the ones we move toward. When we are listened to it creates us, makes us unfold and expand."

Dr. Karl Augustus Menninger
American Psychiatrist and Psychoanalyst

The Harvard Man
(As told by Charles Windwehen)

Each year in early December our city has a combination employee service awards and Holiday Season banquet. We have a dinner, awards and then a dance later. All employees are invited, along with spouses, or guests. My wife and I almost always go, and stay for the dance. My wife is a good dancer, and loves to dance. I can get by on the dance floor, and together we do okay. The Council and most of the Department Directors rarely stay for the dance.

At the 2001 banquet, I was walking across the large dance floor. It was getting pretty late in the evening. One of our employees ran up to me and started talking. He was an older Hispanic man from our Water/Wastewater Department. I was pretty sure he was either an equipment operator or driver, but not a mid-level manager.

His tone was very sincere. He might have had a beer or two, but he certainly wasn't inebriated. He knew that I was the Assistant City Manager.

The first thing he said was, "You look like a Harvard Man out there." (Referring to the dance floor.)

I immediately wondered what image this man had of a "Harvard Man," and asked something like "What do you mean?"

He said, "Well, you always dress so sharp and you and your wife look so good out there dancing."

I said, "Thank you, my wife is a good dancer and makes

me look good."

He said, "No, I just want you to know that I think that you are all right."

Then he said with a laugh, "When I grow up, I want to be just like you."

I was stunned by his simple honesty and the sincere compliment. I know this man did not have a high level job, and I doubted that he had much money in his family. I told him that I was one of seven children. I grew up poor on a small farm in Gonzales County, that I was taught to do your best in school and work hard. That was the way to get a good job, and that was what I had done.

This is what I believe and this is what I want to believe about that incident: It is true that I always try to look professional at work and at City events. But I don't think that this was about the suit I wore. It was incredible to me that this man felt comfortable to come up and talk to me and say what he said. Because of my upbringing I have always treated all persons with respect, no matter their station in life. I had many laboring jobs in my life before working for the City. I make it a point to attend employee retirements and other employee functions and talk with Department employees when I get the chance. When I do this, perhaps they realize that I am just another person, not that different from them, and that I hold the job I do because of my training and experience.

We have over 600 full-time employees plus many part-time employees. I am sure that there are some that I never meet. I have learned from our City Manager, Denny Arnold, and from my Human Resources Director how important it is to meet the employees when you get the chance. Treating people with respect was something I learned at home.

Incidentally, I might actually have had an opportunity

to attend Harvard after graduating from Texas A&M. I received an invitation from their Graduate School of Business with promise of financial aid, but I didn't want to get that far from home, so I didn't pursue that opportunity. That employee had no way of knowing that, and I didn't share that with him.

You don't need a Harvard MBA to learn how important it is as a manager to treat all employees with respect and let your employees know that you're a regular person, just like them. This is what this employee's comments brought home to me.

KEY INSIGHT
Treat others as you want to be treated is just as true at the City as it is in Sunday School. Appreciating people as individuals is not only good manners, but it is a sure way to build goodwill in the workplace.

"The first responsibility of a leader is to define reality. The last is to say thank you. In between the two the leader must become a servant and a debtor. That sums up the progress of an artful leader."

Max DePree in *Leadership is an Art*

Food Chain
(As told by Mike Tanner)

The animal pound that one of my cities operated was so bad, I had to demolish it. In an effort to save money, improve animal housing, make it more humane and improve the image of animal control, I went through an alternatives analysis process and the city ultimately entered into a contract with a local veterinarian to shelter, place and when necessary euthanize animals.

Compared to what the city had been spending the vet was incredibly inexpensive. Shelter fees were now extremely low and euthuanization fees were even lower. The council loved the fact that the contract was staying local and that I had achieved efficiencies in the budget. The community loved "Doc" and adoptions went way up. I was extremely happy until I began to get a few complaints.

A number of citizens began commenting that "Doc" was driving a pick-up loaded with animal carcasses. They and their children thought it gruesome and weird.

I approached the vet the next day. He was docking puppy tails with razor scissors and offered me an opportunity to participate. While declining I told him I was there to investigate a complaint that he was driving around town with a load of animal carcasses.

Without looking up from his task he said it was true and didn't think it was anybody's business what he did with the animal carcasses.

I reminded him that he served the City and couldn't do just anything he felt like.

Silence.

I asked him where he was taking the animal carcasses.

He told me he took them to the alligator farm nearby.

I couldn't believe it! I said, "What? The alligators eat them?"

He said two words, "Food Chain."

I asked him if the chemical used to euthanize the animals affected the alligators.

"What chemicals?" he responded.

He then proceeded to show me how he euthanized the animals. He took an animal to his shop floor, petted it, put water on it, and quickly electrocuted it with an electrical cord.

Shocked at the process I asked him if that was considered humane.

Again, I got a short answer. "It's quick, and it's painless, and after all, dead is dead."

From his demeanor I could tell he was getting quite frustrated with me.

Nonetheless I asked him if his procedure was even legal.

In a louder voice he reminded me that in our state the courts used essentially the same process to deal with the folks it could not rehabilitate. He made it very clear he was the vet, not me, and knew what he was required to do. He was quite offended that I would question his judgment.

After he had calmed down a moment he asked me if I thought his facility was better than the one the City demolished.

I said, "Yes." (There was no question about that.)

He asked me if I thought the animals he sheltered were

better cared for than before.

I told him, "Yes." (In fact Doc loved animals and while in his custody they were treated very well.)

He asked me if the adoption rate had improved since he had served the City.

I told him, "Yes." (It had significantly improved.)

He asked me if the City's cost of animal control had not decreased significantly.

I told him, "Yes." (Numbers don't lie. It was a fact.)

Then Doc said, "Well, it seems to me that you have a decision to make. It is my way or the highway. Read the contract. I am responsible for all aspects of the operation, and by your own admission every area has improved. Do you want to continue contracting with me or go back to providing animal shelter services in-house?"

Doc knew he had me. (He was the only vet in town!)

As a professionally trained City Manager I applied my knowledge, wisdom and experience to this challenge.

I focused on the complaints, identified the problem, considered the alternative (my own shelter, diminished care, higher costs, a declining adoption rate, an increased number of complaints) and did the only thing a good City Manager could do.

I asked him to cover the carcasses when he took them to the alligator farm.

He looked directly at me, gave me a "You Bet," produced a large tarp, and the issue was never revisited while I was City Manager there.

Of course this was many years ago; the alligator farm closed a long time ago and 'Doc" has passed on.

I am sure animal control has been on the decline in that city ever since.

KEY INSIGHT

Good managers always have to balance the public good with available resources. They have a bias for action and never lose sight of the desired outcome. As times change, so do standards and what is considered acceptable. Stay current.

"Jefferson. The Jefferson City council is attacking the high cost of living by allowing the city marshal fifty cents a head for killing dogs, instead of twenty-five cents, as heretofore."

From the Texas Municipal League archives,
1917, Volume 4, Number 5, Page 178.

Backing In
(As told by Mike Conduff)

Nothing brings out a crowd to a council meeting in a university community like ordinances dealing with parking or pets. In this case from years ago, the city was following the then national trend of restricting pit bulls within the corporate limits. While the community had not had any tragedies several folks had petitioned the council to take action.

Of course those folks did not appear the night the ordinance was up for adoption. Instead the chambers were packed with folks who were pit bull owners and lovers. Without appearing biased it is fair to say that some folks who fancy this breed share some of the characteristics of their pets. Consequently, during public comment the speakers were loud, aggressive and tenacious.

The Council listened respectfully to all sides and then passed the ordinance that would prohibit pit bulls being kept inside the city limits.

The crowd was rowdy and disappointed, and it took the efforts of the police officers in attendance to encourage them to disperse in a somewhat orderly manner so the council could finish its business.

The balance of the meeting went reasonably quickly, and after finishing up some paper work, I left the building in the company of the Public Works Director.

We each had assigned parking spaces in the employee

lot in the alley behind the municipal building. We were just unlocking our cars in the dark alley when all of a sudden three older model pickups screamed around the corner and blocked us both in. In the back of each of the trucks were several large dogs – clearly pit bulls!

With lights left on and loud engines left running, the doors to the trucks flew open and some equally large men jumped out. "We want to talk to you!" they hollered.

My life flashed before my eyes, and my first thought was to throw myself in my car and escape. But I had parked head first in the space and could not leave without backing out. The trucks had pulled in behind me, effectively preventing a backing maneuver. My only choice was to put a game face on the situation and confront it head on. With heart pounding I smiled, stuck my hand out and said, "Hi, I'm Mike. How can I help you boys?"

Fully expecting to be beat up or to serve as the appetizer to the dog's evening meal, I was especially surprised to hear the leader say, "We want you to pet our dogs so you can see how gentle they are."

Under the circumstances there wasn't much else to do. And, after a half hour of being slobbered on (by the dogs) and listening to why pit bulls make the best pets (by the owners) I was finally able to escape in one piece. Remarkably, the men had been very nice, as had the pit bulls. I once again relearned that you cannot judge an owner by his dog.

Still, to this day, I always back into a parking space – or at least position myself so I can make a quick exit. As a City Manager you never know when a group will really want to feed you to the dogs!

"If being a City Manager was easy anyone could do it and it wouldn't pay very much!"

Mike Conduff

The Seventh Son of a Seventh Son (As told by Kyle McCain)

I was the second City Manager in Valley Mills, a small town in central Texas. With only a very small staff many duties fell to the City Manager, the oddest of which was serving as the "Public Weigher."

The only scales in town were located at city hall so when one of the area ranchers took a calf to the locker plant to be slaughtered they first brought it to city hall. There I gave them the gross weight of the truck and trailer and calf. After unloading the calf they would return to City Hall and get the tare weight, that of the empty trailer or truck. With simple subtraction they would then have the weight of the calf.

This process cost the rancher 25 cents, which I was entitled (by ordinance) to keep as a benefit of the job.

One rancher, who came to town each month, was known in the area as the "Seventh Son of a Seventh Son." He was also known to have the "Gift." His specialty was removing warts by touching them.

For years I had been plagued with a small wart on my nose. For the entire time that I was the weigher and knew this Seventh Son of a Seventh Son I never charged him the regular quarter, but instead he traded a nose rub for his weighing.

During that entire time I never had the wart return.

When I left Valley Mills, I went to Overton as the City

Manager. Within two months of leaving and losing my monthly nose rub, the wart grew so fast that I had to have it surgically removed.

KEY INSIGHT

There are very few "perks" in the public sector. Remember that whatever you do might quite likely show up on the front page. However, when the job allows special experiences and opportunities, be sure to experience them.

"Whatever you are, be a good one!"

Abraham Lincoln

Lakeway – Urban Deer Capital of Texas (As told by Dave Benson)

L akeway is the Urban Deer Capital of Texas. The deer are everywhere. They roam the golf courses in droves and invade the manicured lawns of the residents at will. They eat flowers and strip the leaves from all of the lowest limbs of trees.

Far from being cute this is a true dilemma. Of course the residents consider this is a "city" problem, and in response the city tried many, many solutions that had worked in other urban locations.

One of our best humane solutions was to trap and relocate the deer. We hired a professional at a pretty fair country expense to set up bait stations and drop nets on the feeding deer. They were then trailered to locations that were very desirous of receiving the bonanza of this natural resource.

In March of 2001 twenty-four deer died during their relocation from Lakeway to a national forest in East Texas due to delays in their release from the trailer in which they were being transported. I was made aware of the incident the following day and assisted a game warden from the incident area with the investigation, providing details as I knew them.

About two months later, I was called by the investigator to provide "wrap up" details for his report. When he began asking for my "full name" and "social security number" I began to get suspicious. I asked him why he needed such information and whether he was considering me for legal action.

He said, "Yes, of course."

They were going to file Class B misdemeanor charges against me, as the responsible agent for the City of Lakeway, for inhumane treatment of deer.

I went into semi-shock at that point.

He went on to say that since I had signed on behalf of the City for the permit to trap and relocate the deer, I was responsible for the deer dying.

We all learn things we never dreamed would be part of our lives as City Managers. Urban deer overpopulation is the top of my list of these things. Over the past eight years, I have learned more than I ever dreamed about urban whitetail deer, their behavior, deer trapping, moving deer in trailers, when to trap, when not to trap, State Laws, methods of dealing with deer overpopulation. But in my study of the applicable State laws, it never occurred to me that wildlife law enforcement would attempt to hold me responsible for an event that happened 150 miles away from Lakeway, where I was asleep in my bed at the time of the incident.

Within two weeks I was notified by Texas Parks and Wildlife that they wanted me to appear at a specific Travis County municipal court for magistration. They went on to say that in regard to my being a public official they would forgo the customary arrest procedure!

So off I went at the appointed hour with my Mayor to face the judge. I went through the magistration procedure, was finger printed at court and released on $2,000 bond. Throughout all this, I was suffering a lot of mortification and my Mayor was as indignant as he could get away with in his remarks to the TP&W arresting officer.

That afternoon, we got the first call from the media, followed by a story in the Austin paper, followed by about a week of hearing of my arrest in the newspapers, on TV and the morning radio talk shows. I can honestly say my "15 minutes of fame" came as my story was featured on the Bob and Sammy morning radio show, including call-ins from all walks of life and all viewpoints regarding the incident and subsequent arrest.

The City Council and residents were 150% supportive of me during all of this. The Council hired the best criminal defense attorney in Austin who quickly pointed out to the County Attorney of San Jacinto County that they had no case against me, as to prove me guilty under the Penal Code they would have to show that I acted knowingly with criminal intent.

As a result no formal charges were ever filed against me. It is my understanding that the State Law in question is going to be changed to go after deer trappers, not city officials. The game warden investigator failed to fully explore the deer trapper's side of the story, which would have showed that the deer deaths were, in fact, largely the responsibility of the receiving agency.

And, to put a happy ending to my short career in the Texas criminal justice system, (and to allow me to even tell this story!) the statute of limitations has finally run out on the offense.

Is there a moral to my story? Perhaps the lesson would be that as a City Manager you will frequently be asked to act on behalf of your City. You will do so many times and sooner or later Murphy's Law will catch up with you. Being a City Manager is kind of like any dangerous sport, if you do it often and long enough, sooner or later something bad will happen to you.

In my case, to my fellow City Managers, my friends, and my golfing buddies, and yes, even my extended family, I will forever be known as "Dave, the Deerslayer!"

KEY INSIGHT

In public service, virtually no good deed goes unpunished. As the CEO of the municipality, the manager is the target for those who would seek to hold someone (anyone!) accountable.

"Champions are pioneers and pioneers get shot at. The companies that get the most from champions, therefore, are those that have rich support networks so their pioneers will flourish. This point is so important it's hard to overstress. No support system, no champions. No champions, no innovations."

Tom Peters, *In Search of Excellence*

The City Manager Must Be Flexible (As told by Fritz Lanham)

One of my mentors in Lubbock was City Manager H. P. Clifton. I was one of his administrative aides way back in the mid-nineteen fifties. I became his administrative assistant and later Assistant City Manager.

Mr. Clifton usually had several administrative aides; he called us his "boys." We were all aspiring City Managers. He frequently gave us advice on things we should do as City Managers and he also suggested things we should not do—among them were starting a municipal bus system and building a zoo.

In the early 60's, Mr. Clifton left Lubbock and became City Manager in Abilene. I came to Baytown about the same time.

One day, I read in the newspaper that Abilene had passed a bond election and among the items approved by the voters were a bus system and a zoo.

I couldn't wait to call Mr. Clifton and remind him of his advice to us trainees.

He said, "That's correct. I did advise you to stay out of the bus business and not to build a zoo."

He went on, "But I also told you that a City Manager must be flexible. The council and the community wanted a bus system and a zoo, so now they will get what they asked for!"

KEY INSIGHT

It is a time tested adage in City and County management circles that after you have given your best advice to the governing body and they vote on the matter, whatever they decide (as long as it is not illegal, unethical or immoral) you need to help them accomplish it.

Buford Watson used to say it this way, "There will be times you do not understand the direction the council is going. In fact you may adamantly disagree with them. Nonetheless you will find that they generally reflect the attitudes of the people who elected them, and ultimately the community. If what they ask you to do is not illegal, immoral or unethical, then do it – or resign your position and move on to another community."

"In the confrontation between the stream and the rock, the stream always wins – not through strength, but by perseverance."

H. Jackson Brown
Author of *Life's Little Instruction Book*

Crossing the Boundary
(As told by Jack Hamlett)

My first City Manager position was in a South Carolina city during the late 1970's and I was the first City Administrator for the city. The population of the city was nearly equally divided 50% black and 50% white. Therefore, the subject of racial relations was a significant element in the success of my position.

Soon after starting my position, the mother of one of the black councilmen died. Another black councilman was owner of the funeral home which was handling the service, so I asked him if it would be appropriate for me to attend the funeral service. He replied yes and told me he would meet me at the church.

When I arrived, he escorted me to a seat. Then I observed that I was the only white attending. As a newcomer to the city, I wasn't sure how my action would be perceived by other city leaders.

In retrospect, I believe the experience was significant for me personally and for my position as the first professional manager in this community. First, the situation helped me demonstrate my respect for the councilman without any regard to race. Secondly, the experience helped me appreciate firsthand being in such situations.

Following the incident, the councilman and I developed a strong personal respect for each other, which lasted throughout my five years in the position. With this relationship as a basis, I was successful demonstrating a professional trust with the leadership in the black community and in developing the value of a professional manager who serves all citizens. This enabled me to be a positive advocate for equal opportunities for both the citizens and city employees.

Even though I did not think about the consequences at the time, I sincerely believe the experience helped me become a better professional and be better prepared to encounter similar issues which have occurred during my career.

KEY INSIGHT
Respect for others, irrespective of position, wealth, race, gender, or influence is critical to engendering trust, and trust is a key component of change. The profession of city management works because people know the city manager will do the right thing for them, no matter where they live, what kind of car they drive, how much money they make or what color they are.

"I have learned that people will forget what you said, people will forget what you did, but people will never forget how you made them feel."

Maya Angelou
Poet

Get the Health Out
(As told by Joe Pence)

Back in 1969 when I was first starting in the City Management profession in Wichita Falls, we were having budget meetings with the staff. Gerald Fox was City Manager back then. Randy Hempling and I were administrative assistants and had been employed about six months.

It was very late one night (about 11:30 pm) in the conference room at the long conference table. Jerry Dunn, Assistant City Manager, Joe Watts, Director of Finance, Jerry Fox, Randy and I were all sitting around the table. Randy and I were sitting down toward the end of the table. Joe Watts was in charge of the roll-out file folder that contained all of the individual department's budget requests.

It had been a long night and Randy and I had, quite frankly, fallen asleep. All of a sudden, without warning, a piercing voice, quite loudly said, "Get the Hell Out!"

I woke up immediately and asked Randy, "What did he say?" Randy indicated, "He said, get the hell out." I simply got up and headed toward the door – thinking my career as a city manager had ended almost before it started.

Mr. Fox said, "Where are you going?"

I said, "Didn't you tell me to get the hell out?"

He said, "No, I said, get the <u>health</u> out. Get the health out of the budget!"

I was embarrassed, but extremely happy to get another chance.

> **KEY INSIGHT**
> Being a Manager requires physical as well as mental strength and stamina. Staying in good shape and taking care of your health is a critical success factor in the public arena, and in late night budget sessions.
>
> "Take care of your body with steadfast fidelity. The soul must see through these eyes alone, and if they are dim, the whole world is clouded."
>
> Johann Wolfgang von Goethe
> German Dramatist

Whose Side are You On?
(As told by Nick Finan)

While I was the City Planner for Lufkin, a gentleman came in asking about operating a mechanic shop out of his garage. I explained to him that zoning prevented that and explained the process he would have to go through to get it changed.

He was unhappy that he couldn't just do it. He always felt his property was his property and the government should not be involved. As he kept trying to persuade me that he did not need a zone change, he only got more irate at my resolve to insist he seek a zone change or just not do it.

I suspect he knew his neighbors would object and his location was one that the P&Z and City Council would not be too tolerable about allowing a mechanic shop to go in.

After failing at all logic he became abusive, attacking my youth and my education; indicating that my not having learned life through the School of Hard Knocks made me less a person.

He finally ended by saying that it was hard to believe that the government was controlling his property. "I fought in World War II against Commies like you!" he exclaimed.

I almost asked him which country he had fought for – Germany or Japan – but knew that would have been a career ending move.

KEY INSIGHT

Abuse by those we serve is often a bitter reward. The same person that attacks you today for not allowing them to violate the rules will be the person that tomorrow castigates you for allowing their neighbor to do so. Thick skin and a sense of humor is a great asset in public service!

"Standing in the middle of the road is very dangerous; you get knocked down by traffic from both sides."

Margaret Thatcher
Former Prime Minister

What the Hex?
(As told by Kelvin Knauf)

In one of my early communities the City was sued by a citizen for stopping her in traffic and arresting her for not having her children in seat belts in a moving vehicle.

The city, of course, won the lawsuit – it was actually dismissed at the district court on summary judgment. The citizen then appealed to the Court of Appeals in New Orleans.

As the City Manager I was designated to sit at the table with our attorney and so was witness to a most interesting exchange.

Before the judge came into the courtroom, the citizen's husband, who was a medical professional, approached the City's attorney and presented him with a voodoo doll, explaining, "We are going to put a Hex on you."

Our attorney never skipped a beat. He looked at the voodoo doll in his hand and said, "I'm starting to feel worse already. Who do I sue? You?"

The doctor just turned and walked away.

In any case The Hex must not have taken. The Court affirmed the City's actions and assessed the court costs to the citizen.

"I have been wounded but not yet slain. I shall lie here and bleed awhile. Then I shall rise and fight again. The title of champion may from time to time fall to others more than ourselves. But the heart, the spirit, and the soul of champions remains in us."

Vince Lombardi
Coach

The Nuclear Warning
(As told by Joe Pence)

While I was serving as City Manager in Henrietta, Texas one of the projects that the City completed was installation of a warning siren system. Since this was shortly after the Wichita Falls tornado of 1979, it was important to the citizens and to my Emergency Management Coordinator (EMC).

When the installation of the radio-controlled sirens was complete the last step was to set the radio frequencies for remote activation. We had had a little difficulty getting the settings correctly coded but thought we were finished.

That next night a storm blew in about midnight and suddenly the sirens went off. I was up out of bed and sitting behind my desk at City Hall before the three-minute warning siren stopped.

The second person at City Hall was the EMC, who was in a state of extreme stress. He had correctly recognized the siren's warning as the "Nuclear Attack Warning." He had immediately turned on his radio to the designated station for emergency warnings for further instructions and immediately heard the alert tone being broadcast on the radio.

In those few moments before the tone ended and the station announced that familiar, "This has been a test of the early warning system" he had been convinced by the combination of the siren's wail and the radio tone that we were under attack. I have never seen such an anxious person before or since.

We later learned that siren had been set off by a distant radio signal that had bounced in under the clouds of the storm. These radio signals triggered our radio-controlled siren that had not yet been correctly set. The radio station test was merely a coincidence.

If you know how "focused" an EMC is, then you know how funny this really is; although I have always been impressed that even believing a nuclear attack was occurring the EMC left his home and his family to come to work to serve the citizens of Henrietta.

KEY INSIGHT

Duty is a difficult task master. Public servants regularly put the well-being of the community and its citizens ahead of their own safety or that of their loved ones.

"Greater love has no one than this: to lay down one's life for one's friends."

John 15:13
NIV

Caught Late in the Office
(As penned by Gary Brown)

Came to work without much to do,
Fixed coffee, read the paper and shined my shoe.
Waited for the day to end so I could go,
The work here this week was really slow.

About the time I was ready to close the door,
On this day which had been a bore,
Here came a citizen with a mean look;
The other door I should have took.

The day got livelier and overtime I was now on,
My chance to go home early was now gone.
I heard an awful tale about how he was cheated;
About his water this citizen was truly heated.

The meter wasn't read and he had not used that much,
This conversation was not one you would call Dutch.
When he could no longer talk or carry on,
I really wished that I had been gone.

I explained that the meter usually was true,
But that I would re-read the meter is what I would do.
He agreed for me to do this and do it now;
He wanted to watch so he would know how.

I went to his house and found the meter,
Removed the lid like any meter reader.
Looked at the numbers and they were more,
He wasn't going to be happy I knew for sure.

Told him he had used some additional water;
He was showing to be hotter and hotter!
The leak detection hand was moving fairly fast,
If I told him this I might not last.

Built up my courage and pointed out the leak;
He just about reached his temperature peak.
No way was the meter showing what really was;
This man was stirred up, he was a buzz.

I asked if he had a faucet or shower that wouldn't
    turn off?
If I had left a minute sooner I could be playing golf!
The reply I received cannot be put into print,
My knowledge to him I shouldn't have lent.

We went into his house to take a look;
The amount of water he was losing would fill a brook.
The kitchen sink was half-full, the shower had a
    nice stream too;
I thought I would tell him what he might do.

I thought about how this man had ranted and raved;
Why should I care about what water he saved?
Then when I left the house I saw a yard faucet
    with water running through...
Hmm, let this man decide what to do!

KEY INSIGHT

Clarifying the differing roles of customers and owners is difficult in the abstract, and especially so in the heat of the moment. When the same person is both an owner and a customer, it is important to focus on the issue itself. The private sector clearly knows the difference between a stockowner and a customer, but that line is very blurry in the public sector. No matter what, managers must give exemplary customer service.

"Just because it is hard does not mean that it is impossible. When the going gets tough, the tough get going."

Bill Scott
Former Pittsburg, KS Fire Chief,
and one of Mike's Mentors

Democracy at the Doorstep

Lessons in Life from High Grass (As told by Bryan Easum)

Approximately 20 years ago, I was City Administrator in a small community in rural Nebraska. Since we had no code enforcement personnel, that task fell to me. The Mayor and Council were very concerned about community appearance, so every Friday I drove the community and issued a few notices on mostly minor violations.

One Friday, I sent a letter about high grass to a citizen. I did not know the gentleman or anything about his circumstances. It turned out the owners were an elderly gentleman and his wife in their eighties.

Upon receiving the letter, the owner was very upset that he had let the lawn get out of hand to the point that he had gotten a letter from the City. Despite the protestations of his wife, he went out into the hot sun that day, and began to mow the yard.

While mowing, he suffered a heart attack and died.

I had a visit from several neighbors the next Monday. They came in quite angry, but calmed down once they saw how sorry I was and read the copy of the letter that I had sent, which was quite polite and solicitous.

I have often thought about this individual, and although I did not see anything I would have done differently in the situation, it has been a lifelong reminder that not everyone who has a code violation or pays a bill late is a person that deserves harsh treatment from the City.

A little empathy goes a long way in influencing how those "occasional" problem citizens are treated by the City, and how they in turn view their City government.

KEY INSIGHT

Often being the CEO is emotionally demanding. It is important to do the right thing all of the time so that when something difficult occurs, you can fall back on the knowledge that your action was appropriate given the circumstances.

"The obvious is that which is never seen until someone expresses it simply."

Kahlil Gibran

The No Brainer
(As told by Mike Conduff)

While the objectives of the local paper and the city to inform the citizens of the community are to some degree the same, both parties clearly have their own interests. Reporters want to retain journalistic integrity and win the Pulitzer, and City Managers and Public Information Officers want their message written in the most positive light – particularly when the subject is a difficult one.

After weeks of public debate on an exceedingly difficult and contentious community financing issue for a local economic development initiative, and its concomitant press coverage, the council adjourned into a final executive session with their most excellent city attorney. Based on the legal alternatives laid out for them, and after much council conversation, the Mayor believed he understood the thrust of the council's thoughts.

Recognizing that how this issue would be framed by the locally owned newspaper would be critical, the Mayor suggested that he and I go visit with the News Editor directly. This would give us a chance to tell the city's side of the story and hopefully get the city a bit more consideration when the reporter went to write his article.

I dutifully called up the Editor and made the appointment. As this was an unusual occurrence he wanted to know what was up. I told him generally what the subject was and that the Mayor would lay it all out when we got there.

At the appointed time I drove over to the newspaper headquarters and was ushered into the Editor's office. We chatted about the University's sports teams, golf, and the weather for 20 or 30 minutes while waiting on the Mayor. It was a fine dance of trivialities that we both executed to perfection. He wanted to know what was going on and I was determined that the Mayor would deliver the message.

Eventually the Editor's secretary came in and said that the Mayor had called, wasn't going to be able to make it, and had asked me to go ahead and fill in the Editor.

I was relatively young in my career, and so, ignoring the warning tingle up my spine, I laid out the situation, pointed out the alternatives the city had (most of which were not good!) and shared with the Editor the item that the council would consider on their agenda at the next meeting.

A very good newspaperman, the Editor asked really pointed questions, which I answered as fully as I could. As we concluded the session, which I naively thought had gone exceedingly well considering the circumstances, he said, "So, all things considered you believe the City's action here is a no brainer?"

I replied, "Well, if you take everything into account, and recognizing that the situation is very difficult, and that reasonable people can disagree on the item, then, yes, it's a no brainer."

The above the fold headline the next day was, "City Manager Says Bailout is No Brainer."

My phone rang all day with callers questioning my sanity, my pedigree and my basic right to life, and the council meeting the next Tuesday was packed. In fact it had to be relocated to a gymnasium to accommodate the largely hostile crowd. One after another citizens came to the podium to tell the council that "the %#&! City Manager was the one without brains!

What would have been a very difficult decision for the council became almost untenable for them. Ultimately, after more weeks of controversy, the council did vote to pursue the financing, which the years have proven to be an incredibly wise direction.

While the council was ultimately courageous, the pain of being skewered by a hostile crowd for doing what I had been asked to do by my bosses left me with such scars that to this very day, the phrase "it's a no brainer" makes me break out in a cold sweat!

KEY INSIGHT

City councils are always vulnerable to swaying in the wind of public opinion. It often does not matter as much what the facts are as what people's perceptions are and what they are saying. Private commitments are nonbinding when a crowd shows up at a council meeting.

As a public manager, when you climb, or crawl, or are pushed out on the limb, it is wise to make sure the chainsaws are not being warmed up behind you.

Old sayings get to be old sayings because they are so often true. "Don't shoot the messenger" continues to be uttered, so be careful about being the point person on issues that are community divisive.

The ancient mariners knew that the only time a whale was in danger of being harpooned was when it came to the surface and began spouting off.

"Someone asked me once to describe the role of city manager. I said it was like being the quarterback in the last two minutes of a professional football game, with your team down by six. The ball is on the twenty, and you need to score a touchdown to win. The only difference for a city manager is your own team members are allowed to tackle you, and take great delight in doing so."

John Menario
Former City Manager of Portland, Maine

Can't Put it to Bed
(As told by Warren Driver)

In the mid 80's, I was selected as the new City Manager in a prominent old East Texas City. The city was renovating an ornate 1920's school building as the new central library and was about half finished.

The Mayor informed me, "Warren, this is something you need to get a handle on right away. Construction progress is painfully slow. The contractor is at odds with the engineer. The engineer blames the architect and they all, in turn, point fingers at each other. In the interim, the building is not being built."

When I arrived early the next month, they had arranged a 9 a.m. meeting on site with the contractor, engineer and architect. We began to make good progress. Within a few weeks, the architect said, "I am not coming to any more meetings unless there is an emergency." Within a few more weeks, the engineer dropped out and said, "Please call if I can help. I have to earn a living." In spite of this, we continued to make good progress. Within a few months, we were ready for a dedication ceremony. The building was gorgeous. The library board was delighted. The mayor and council were complimentary and a grand time was had by all. Finally, I thought, after weeks of anxiety (with the council and library board wondering if the new City Manager was up to the task and the City Manager wondering as well) here it was: sweet success at last.

Within the same month, I got a call from the Mayor early one Monday morning. "Warren," he said, "There is a pile of pigeon dung just a few feet in front of the main entrance to the library." The Mayor explained that one of the library's most prominent backers had called him about an hour earlier.

"We must do something quickly," the Mayor said.

I went immediately to the new library and found the situation just as it was reported. The problem was obvious; the pigeons were using a beam within the entrance alcove as a roost. I called the Public Works Director to see if he could find some way to remedy the situation.

After a quick examination, he said, "I have got the answer. We have some matching metal flashing we can install which will render the perch too slick for the pigeons."

Late the next day, the metal flashing was installed in an excellent workmanlike fashion. It looked good. Problem solved. I checked on it for the next week. No more pigeon dung.

Very quickly, other problems occupied my attention and I forgot about the library pigeons.

Less than three weeks later, an irate Mayor called again. "These pigeons are going to be our undoing," he said. "There is more pigeon dung in front of the library—this time about 15 feet in front of the main entrance."

I went immediately to the library. The problem was obvious. The pigeons had moved to a less desirable exterior exposed beam. Upon returning to the office, I called the Mayor as requested and reported my findings. Neither of us had an immediate answer, but the Mayor said, "I am not sure, but I believe the P.D. has some pellet guns they use for snakes, varmints and pests."

I thought, "These library pigeons surely qualify as pests."

I called the Police Chief and discussed my dilemma with him. He said they did have some pellet guns and were in need of target practice and would be delighted to address the problem.

I was unaware that an officer in the local ASPCA lived a short distance from the library. In about a week, the City Secretary received a call threatening the city with a lawsuit if our pigeon control program was not immediately re-evaluated.

After consultation with our City Attorney, I determined we should look into an alternative approach. In conversation with our library architect about another matter, I brought up the matter of the pigeons. He said, "I don't have the answer, but I know who does." I was put in touch with the East Texas pigeon expert.

A few weeks and a few thousand dollars later, we had electrified wires strung along every possible pigeon perch on the new library. In the interim, public works had an early morning ritual of scooping up pigeon dung.

The electrified wires worked. No more pigeon problem.

Finally, I had put this library problem to bed and could go on to other things that needed attention.

This worked very well for nearly a year. At the next big rain event, the assistant librarian noticed a leak in the children's section. A call to the contractor resulted in the involvement of the engineer, the architect and the bonding company. None wanted to be involved and was sure the fault lay elsewhere. In the next few weeks, more rain came, resulting in damage to some of the children's books. Now, this is a flat roof and everyone knows all flat roofs leak—it just depends on the amount and intensity.

Upon personal inspection, it was determined that the roof leak was likely caused by one of the ladder legs used by the installers of the electrified wires. The wire installer had a section of the roof cut out, at his expense, which showed improper installation of roofing components at a previously unknown date.

By the way, while on the roof of the library, I happened to bump into one of the electrified wires, which we had neglected to disconnect before climbing onto the roof. I understood why the pigeons abandoned the whole block.

As far as I know, there has never been a final resolution to the continuing problems with that building. It never has been put to bed.

KEY INSIGHT

It is generally the little things that cause the manager the most aggravation. Intellectually we know we should focus on the major issues, because in reality those are the ones that can truly impact the future of the community. Often though, in order to survive managers must balance the critical trivial with the non-urgent important.

"When everything seems to be going against you, remember that the airplane takes off against the wind, not with it."

Henry Ford, Founder
Ford Motor Company

The Squirrel Cage
(As told by Ray Kendall)

When I was the City Manager of a small Texas town with its own electric utility, we were having a major problem with electrical transformers blowing out because squirrels would run along the wires to the transformers and short them out.

After discussions with the electric power supplier they advised the town to purchase squirrel guards for the electric transformers.

Staff did the requisite research, and determined that the cost would be about $15,000 to protect the transformers. We then asked the Council to approve this non-budgeted expense so that we could avoid replacing the transformers, which were blowing quite frequently at a cost of $750 to $1000 each.

The Council for the most part was in favor of this purchase, but the Mayor was strongly opposed, and not surprisingly the purchase was not approved.

As predicted we continued to experience electric transformers being blown with no relief in sight. About two weeks later the Mayor walked into my office carrying a paper bag.

The previous night the electric transformer had blown behind his house and he and his neighbors had no electricity for several hours until we were able to replace the transformer.

The Mayor then suggested to me that we needed to put the request to purchase the squirrel guards back on the agenda.

He then opened the paper bag and showed me a dead squirrel that had been killed by shorting out the power transformer and had fallen into the Mayor's back yard.

The request to purchase squirrel guards was unanimously approved at the next Council meeting.

KEY INSIGHT

Issues take on a whole new perspective when an elected official is personally impacted. Having citizens tell their stories is another way of cultivating this empathetic perspective as well. If elected officials can understand the issue from the heart of someone they know or respect they will often see it in a different light. All the logic in the world does not replace a good story from a credible source.

"Your representative owes you, not his industry only, but his judgment; and he betrays instead of serves you if he sacrifices it to your opinion."

Edmond Burke
British Orator

The Ugly City Attorney
(As told by James Thurmond)

Once the City Attorney and I had proposed to the City Council that they update the junked car ordinance to comply with state law and to enhance it as an enforcement tool to clean up a few areas in the city. We expected our proposal to be a simple, uncontested action, since most people don't want junked vehicles in their neighborhoods.

However, there was a retired mechanical engineer in town who vigorously opposed any attempts by the city to adopt, strengthen, or update nuisance laws. He always told the City Council that any citizen could seek remedy in district court rather than letting the City pick on citizens by filing on them in Municipal Court.

This retired gentleman, who was about 5' 6" and over 70 years of age, slowly approached the podium during the Council meeting to address the Council about the proposed ordinance. The City Attorney and I both knew that he would be opposed and we expected his typical argument. He surprised us this time as he reviewed his childhood background with cars and how he had learned about cars by working on them in his backyard as a kid.

He then slowly looked down at the floor in front of the Council's semi-circular table and seemed to be gathering his thought for some type of grand summary or conclusion to his remarks. The City Attorney and I sat on opposite ends of the table. He then exclaimed in a very loud voice while pointing first at the City Attorney and then me: "Gentlemen, I want you to know that I have seen many old, junked cars in my life, but never have I seen a car as ugly as the City Attorney, or as ugly as the City Manager! The City Manager and the City Attorney are more of a threat to this community than junked vehicles!"

As he was saying this, he turned first to the City Attorney and pointed straight at him with his forefinger in a slow and deliberate manner, and then he turned to me and pointed at me in the same manner.

The effect of his melodramatic motions and statement was profound. The Mayor was surprised and the Council just sat there wide-eyed and silent. The City Attorney and I also sat there in astonishment.

What were we supposed to say? That we were prettier than a junked car?

Apparently the City Council agreed with the retired gentleman, because the ordinance did not pass! Of course, the City Attorney and I were afraid that there might be an effort to adopt an ordinance controlling ugly city attorneys and city managers and we were prepared to fight that!

This story goes to show that emotional statements and possibly ugly city attorneys and city managers can counteract the best laid plans and ordinances of man!!

KEY INSIGHT

Despite our education and even our altruistic motives, citizens always hold more sway over the council that we do. When emotional statements are used in a council meeting they can neutralize all the rational justification in the world.

"If I were to try to read, much less answer, all the attacks made on me, this shop might as well be closed for any other business. I do the very best I know how – the very best I can; and I mean to keep doing so until the end. If the end brings me out all right, what is said against me won't amount to anything. If the end brings me out wrong, ten angels swearing I was right would make no difference."

Abraham Lincoln

Story Nineteen

The Evaluation Process
(As told by Roger McKinney)

As we all know, annual evaluations are a critical component of good management, although most supervisors
dislike having to do them. Because of this dislike evaluations are generally put off, or in extreme cases a supervisor
will simply mark everyone "satisfactory."

In each of my communities, as part of my City Manager's
responsibilities, I provide an orientation to my department heads on the evaluation process for merit increases.
I strongly encourage the department heads to be honest in
their evaluation. If the employee was deemed marginal or
outstanding in a particular evaluation category, then they
should be rated that way. I do require that if the rating is
above or below a certain level the supervisor must provide
written comments to justify the high or low marks.

The evaluation categories cover such areas as quality
and quantity of work, job knowledge, safety, attendance
and punctuality, initiative, innovation, completion of work,
accuracy, etc.

One department head took my comments quite literally
and on the category "accuracy," which reflects correctness
of work and freedom from errors, noted a substandard
evaluation with the comment, "Doesn't do enough work to
make mistakes."

KEY INSIGHT

In local government the process to terminate an individual is exhausting and fraught with peril – generally for the administrator. In order to guard against abuse of power every step seems to be biased toward the employee. Consequently mediocre and perhaps even non-performance is often tolerated.

Jim Collins' metaphor of the bus sounds good ("Get the right people on the bus, in the right seats on the bus, and the wrong people off the bus") but in local government it is more common just to move folks to the window seats so the folks in the aisles can do the work and the sightseers don't get in the way too much.

"My best definition of character is: knowing the difference between right and wrong, and choosing to do right, irrespective of the cost."

Dr. Rick Rigsby
Pastor, Professor, Professional Speaker,
and one of Mike's Heroes

Money in Your Pocket
(As told by Stan Stewart about
his buddy Mike Conduff)

"It is lonely at the top" is a truism in the City Management business just as it is in many professions. There is only one of you in any given town, and no matter how much you like your Mayor, council members and staff, it is difficult and generally not advisable to confide concerns to them. However innocently it gets repeated (and it will) sooner or later the object of your concern hears about it. That makes the City Manager's professional network and friendships within the business even more important.

In one of Mike's early communities he had a commissioner that simply didn't like the direction the balance of the council was going. Since this commissioner was a lone voice on the council and wasn't able to persuade the other electeds to adopt his views he generally made his displeasure known by confronting Mike and his staff at every opportunity.

It got to the point that whenever Mike saw this individual coming Mike would cringe because he knew the commissioner was going to harangue him about some matter that the council had already decided and that Mike couldn't change.

While visiting Mike in his town one day we were walking the downtown area looking at the CDBG project underway when Mike said, "Let's cross over to the other side

Democracy at the Doorstep

of the street so I can avoid that fellow coming down the sidewalk."

It was the commissioner.

As we switched sides of the street (against the light and through traffic) I was sure I saw the commissioner smirk, so I shared with Mike a mental trick I had learned to use in a similar circumstance.

I figured out the number of times I was likely to see my disgruntled elected official each week, and then divided that into my weekly pay. It worked out to roughly $250 per interaction. (We didn't make much in those days!)

I then played the mental game that each time I had a conversation with my nemesis that I would "make" $250. The key was I could only put the $250 in my pocket if I actually talked to the elected official and he responded in some manner.

This worked so well that over time I would go out of my way to engage the elected official, so I could mentally put $250 in my pocket.

Amazingly, as I sought out the council member, and really worked at hearing him, the elected official came to regard me quite highly and I came to understand his heart for the community.

Although Mike couldn't quite envision the same outcome, he decided it was worth trying.

Sure enough, just making the mental jump from avoiding contact to seeking contact worked wonders for Mike's mental state. While that particular elected official never became a supporter of Mike's or the staff's, Mike's blood pressure sure took a turn for the better, and he didn't have to play dodge-the-traffic ever again.

KEY INSIGHT

You can influence other's behaviors with your own. Since the mind cannot tell the difference between an actual event and an event that is vividly imagined, you can mentally rehearse difficult situations so that when you are actually faced with them your body will know how to react. Olympic athletes do it, gold medal managers should too.

"He that wrestles with us strengthens our nerves, and sharpens our skill. Our antagonist is our helper."

Edmond Burke
British Parliamentarian

What is a City Manager?
(As penned by Gary Brown)

"What is City Management?" the professor did ask,
To prepare the students for future employment was his task.
After much thought the students began to talk,
Through their ideas about city management they began
    to walk.

Many ideas were presented and most were on track,
The Professor was pleased with the student's under-
    standing and tack.
When their thoughts about city management were no
    longer being spoken,
The silence, by the professor, was about to be broken.

"Now that your ideas about city management are known,
I would like knowledge about what a city manager is to
    be sown.
City management and city manager are not the same,
I want you to know what is required when you have this
    name."

The students looked bewildered, and they recognized
What the professor had said, and then they realized
That there really is a difference between the two.
Get the students to think, "Is this what I really want to do?"

The discussion began and different traits came out,
Different students seeing differently during this bout.
None seemed to know what a city manager really was,
Nor exactly what it is that one really does.

One student finally cleared his throat, and speaking very
    clear
You could tell the subject to him was very dear.
"Your ideas are great, but that is not what a city manager
    is,
I know, my dad, for all my life, a city manager job has
    been his."

The student moved to the front of the room to give his
    speech,
This would be an impromptu talk with which he would
    teach
The other students about what they should expect
In this field of combination hands on and high tech.

"Passion, desire and willingness to sacrifice,
Being able to keep a job is sometimes like rolling dice.
You will be living in a house that is made of glass,"
Was the way the student started speaking to the class.

He then went into detail about different parts of the job
"Are you willing to let the job time from the family rob?"
Aspects about the job that the students did not know
Were what the speaker was beginning to them to show.

"You have to be able to lead, follow and get out of the
    way,
Speak to the citizens, watching what you say.

Please the council and employees too,
Is just a part of what you will have to do.

At the end of the day, someone, maybe yourself, will ask,
'Did you do your best at each and every task?
Were the results, whether complete or yet to be done,
The best for all, each and every one?"

There is only one person who is the hardest to please,
It is the person in the mirror that the manager does see.
You will not please everyone no matter how hard you try,
I have seen my dad at day's end just sit down and cry.

Maybe over a job that did not go just right,
Maybe an employee did or said something that caused
    his fright.
Could it have been the disciplining or even dismissal of
    a friend?
That brought this sadness to his day's end?

You will know within yourself when <u>your</u> day does end,
By the feelings that your pride outward does send.
The job is tough but for those who dare
To take on the title, you can show the citizens that you
    care.

Now go forth and apply yourself to your best,
Take the challenge, stand up to the test!
Years from now when your career is winding down
Know within yourself you have helped improve your
    town!"

KEY INSIGHT
There is a difference between what they teach in graduate school about the job of city management and what the job actually entails. Long hours, little thanks, tough decisions are par for the course. Being caught between elected officials, employees and citizens all while subject to the 24/7 media cycle makes public service a challenging, and rewarding career.

"An optimist is someone who goes after Moby Dick in a rowboat, and takes the tartar sauce with him."

Dale Carnegie
Speaker

PS from Gary

"During a spell of being somewhat down and out a few summers ago, the Texas City/County Management Association members were great about calling, sending cards, and in general keeping up with my recovery and with me. I received cards and calls from people whom I really did not know.

I began to realize that even though I did not know these people, they were just as concerned for me as if we were on a first name basis. This shows the strength of the association and the concern our members have for fellow managers going through difficult circumstances."

One of Gary's Jokes –
"Time Flies When You are Having Fun"

A woman was sitting with her doctor after having undergone a series of grueling diagnostic tests.

The doctor said, "Well, Mary, I am afraid I have some pretty bad news. After all of these tests I have to tell you that you really only have about six months to live."

"Oh no, Doctor," said the woman. "Isn't there anything at all that I can do?"

"Well," the doctor replied, "I do recommend that you find a single City Manager in a small town in Texas and marry him."

"Will that cure me?"

"No, but the six months will seem like a really long time."

Two Inch Trees
(As told by Juan Garza)

Jargon is a challenge in any profession, and that is true in local government as well. I have had the pleasure of working in a number of locations with some very well educated elected officials but still try to remember that not everyone speaks the same municipal language.

In one of my early communities the City was fortunate to be awarded a community improvement grant that included putting some streetscape trees in the downtown. One of the conditions of the grant was that we had to prepare bids, have them approved by the city council, advertise in the local paper and then award the bid to the lowest responsible bidder.

While we did not have any tree experts on staff we consulted with the local nursery owner and he suggested that fewer larger trees would be better than more smaller trees because they would have a better root system making them more likely to survive the heat and transplant stress.

He recommended a two inch caliper tree, meaning that the tree would measure about two inches in diameter at about 4 and half feet off of the ground.

This made good sense to staff and we dutifully put that in the specifications that went to council for approval.

At the council meeting one of the members became irate and said, "This is another example of government incompetence. Why in the world would the city want to buy a tree that is only two inches tall? It will take years for it to be big enough to do any good downtown!"

I was very proud of the staff that night for not one of them even cracked a smile while explaining that the two inches meant diameter not height. However, the balance of the council members just roared and never let the incident fade from memory.

KEY INSIGHT

Being respectful of and honoring elected officials is a hallmark of city management. No matter their age, their education, or their station in life, they are elected and therefore to be treated with the respect due the office. Most managers do this, some better than others. The best ones are much admired.

Famous Lawrence, Kansas City Manager Buford Watson once gave a talk where he drew a comparison between two major league baseball players of the day. Both were well known, and one hit .275 while the other hit just shy of .300. The 300 hitter made twice as much as the 275 hitter. Buford pointed out that was only one extra hit in every forty at bats!

He went on to point out that racehorses win by a nose, a marathoner by a step.

You don't have to be twice as good as someone else, just a 5% percent margin will put you out front in this business! Brian Tracy the famous motivational speaker says, "There are no traffic jams on the extra mile."

> "When you are making a success of something, it's not work. It's a way of life. You enjoy yourself because you are making your contribution to the world."
>
> Andy Granatelli,
> *They Call Me Mister 500*

Support Can Be Self Serving
(As told by James Thurmond)

The City Council called a bond election with drainage, water, wastewater, and fire equipment on the ballot. They decided to let each proposal stand on its own, which means that each voter votes yes or no on each of the bond election projects.

This is normal in most bond elections, and the Council did not anticipate any problems.

The Council was committed to the passage of the entire bond package.

In order to ensure a large voter turnout, the Council felt that the volunteer fire department's support would be instrumental. So, a large elevated platform fire truck was included in the package. The Council did this even though the tallest building in town was the old Masonic Lodge which was only two stories.

This particular ladder truck was the same type used by the City of Houston Fire Department for a city of 1.5 million people with multi-storied buildings everywhere.

At the Council's direction I worked hard on selling the bond package to the citizens, and was receiving positive vibes from my audiences. Since I knew the volunteer fire-fighters were working for the package, I was not worried about its passage.

The Council and I were all surprised on Election Day when the only bond package item approved by the voters was the fire ladder truck!

In other words, the City ended up with a ladder truck with doubtful justification for the small city, and did not have drainage, water, or wastewater projects!

KEY INSIGHT

As a manager in the public sector you will need to develop lots of partnerships. Money and public support are difficult to come by and using existing goodwill can be a catapult to success. It is, however, important to make sure that your partners desire the same outcomes as you; otherwise you may wind up on the short end of the vote.

The moral of this story is that you better make sure your bedfellows have the same objective as you. Their objective may be more limited and self-serving than yours, which is big picture focused and for the entire city.

"Our success has really been based on partnerships from the very beginning."

Bill Gates
Microsoft

You Never Make Partner
(As told by Mike Conduff)

One of the really difficult lessons for a City Manager is that there is no financial equity and certainly no security in being the CEO of a municipality. No matter how much money you have saved the town, no matter how much economic development success you have had and no matter how long your tenure, when newly elected officials come onto the council you are in the position of proving yourself all over again. In fact, the way elections work is that people typically run "against" some idea, some occurrence, or even someone, and occasionally you are that someone.

When you are young and full of vim and vigor this is a fun challenge. Sixty and seventy hour weeks are more interesting than burdensome. There is huge satisfaction in helping a newcomer to the council learn the ropes and become successful. It is a joy to help an "anti" become a pro.

However at some point, when the kids are in their adolescent years, and your spouse starts putting a picture of you in their rooms so they can know what their absentee parent looks like, you begin to think about working smarter rather than harder. Trying to be at every conceivable community event to wave the municipality's flag takes its toll.

After teaching the same intro to local government class to the umpteenth elected official who believes they have a mandate because they got a majority of a six or seven percent voter turnout, you run a little short of patience with the same questions you answered joyfully a double handful of years earlier.

Lamenting this situation on the golf course one day with a former elected official who also happened to be one of the successful attorneys in town, he said to me, "You know the problem with your business? You never make partner!"

He went on to explain. "As a young attorney I worked a gazillion hours and really had to sacrifice to get billable hours. Much of the fruits of my labors in those years were going to support the partners in the firm."

He went on, "As I gained stature and tenure, we brought on younger attorneys, and I was able to concentrate in a few more specialized areas. I served on the City Council out of a sense of civic duty. Now I am a partner and have my choice of the cases to work on, and indeed, to some degree how much I work."

Demonstrating that he was choosing golf over work he holed out a nice putt to take the match and then put in the Coup-De-Grace. "Mike, you will always be at the mercy of the ballot box and the latest mistake you or your staff makes. The thing is, you can't take it personally. Most folks who are mad at the City Manager don't even know you are it."

KEY INSIGHT

Being a City Manager is a high calling of a job with the potential to improve the lives of many. Still it is important to recognize that it is just that – a job. Take it for what it offers; the opportunity to serve, and the opportunity to make a difference. Just remember it is not who you are. In the end, you never make partner!

"To serve the public faithfully and please it entirely is simply not possible."

Benjamin Franklin

Friend or Foe?
(As told by Kyle McCain)

As the first City Manager in Overton I had to report to the local newspaper each week on how much I had saved the city that week so it could be printed in the paper. No matter how difficult or complicated the reasoning, it was very important that I be able to show in dollars and cents how efficient the City Manager form of government was.

What I didn't know was that before I was hired the City had had an election to determine whether or not to have a City Manager. The newspaper strongly supported getting a City Manager, against the long-time Mayor's political position.

The election had passed two to one.

A year and a half later, after I had left Overton, the Mayor succeeded in passing a petition to put it to a vote again.

This time much to my satisfaction, it passed three to one.

After the next manager left, the Mayor was able to get another petition to put it to a vote a third time.

This time the community kept the City Manager form by a vote of four to one.

As I understand it, the Mayor retired after that.

What makes this story interesting is that the Mayor and I got along famously on a personal basis, and often he and his wife would volunteer to babysit our toddler.

While his political opinion on the form of government never wavered, he was very good at separating the professional relationship and the personal relationship.

KEY INSIGHT

Over time it is easy to think of oneself in terms of what it is one does. "I am" the City Manager replaces, "I work as" a City Manager, or "I earn a living as" a City Manager, or even, "I serve the community as" a City Manager.

Folks who can separate their roles from their persona are much more likely to be strong emotionally.

"Courage is what it takes to stand up and speak; courage is also what it takes to sit down and listen."

Winston Churchill

The Law Suit
(As told by Ron Cox)

Several years ago I had the opportunity to provide a tour of City Hall, and do a question and answer session for a group of children ranging in ages from six to twelve.

I have learned from having kids of my own that one of the best ways to improve the perception of the city in the community is to treat families well. Many of these kids had one or both parents with them and I hoped that these parents and the other children would go home and tell their families about what a nice city hall the community had and how much they had learned from the tour.

During the discussion we began to talk about Municipal Court, and its functions.

I asked the children, "Who do you think sits behind the big desk?"

An arm went up; I called on the young person, and they answered correctly – "the Judge."

I then asked them, "What does the Judge wear?"

No arms went up for a while, as they were deep in thought.

With some hesitation the arm of a young lady, about seven or eight years old finally did go up.

I called on her, while repeating my question, "What does a judge wear when he is behind the bench?

Very haltingly she offered, "A law suit?

All of the adults laughed, but I quickly commended her

for trying by saying, "Wow, that is a great answer!"

I then went on to explain that our judge always wore a robe.

KEY INSIGHT

Interfacing with children and young adults is one of the great joys of public management. As Art Linkletter (and subsequently Bill Cosby) demonstrated years ago, kids will "say the darndest things!"

Keep a journal of these because there will be moments in your career you need to be reminded of the joys!

"As I have discovered by examining my past, I started out as a child. Coincidentally, so did my brother. My mother did not put all of her eggs in one basket, so to speak: she gave me a younger brother named Russell, who taught me what was meant by 'survival of the fittest.'"

Bill Cosby
Comedian

Marital Status Makes a Difference (As told by Mike Tanner)

I was 24 and single the first time I interviewed for the position of City Manager. The City Council that interviewed me asked me if I was married. I told them that I had a girlfriend, but wouldn't marry her until I was a City Manager.

They asked me if I was serious, (most of them thought that was hilarious) and I made it clear that I was.

I told them we would set a date and marry within six months of my appointment.

I was appointed by a unanimous vote.

After I had accepted the appointment, the mayor informed me the vote was only unanimous because two members of the city council wanted to see if I would really get married.

My wife and I were married five months later and remain married today.

KEY INSIGHT

You never know why elected officials choose the managers they do. Sometimes they stay inside even after pledging that there was no internal candidate. Sometimes they go outside when they clearly have an awesome successor inside. All you can do is evaluate the community, its leadership, its quality of life and its potential. If those add up and you feel like you can deal with the council's individual personalities go for it, even if you aren't married.

"I could never predict with total certainty what the council would do when I was sitting at the dais with them giving them my best advice. When they are acting totally on their own selecting a city manager there is no way to predict who they will choose or why!"

Stan Stewart
Retired City Manager

Cut the Mic
(As told by Craig Lonon)

I had a very nice woman who was a City Commissioner for one of the single member districts in Corsicana, Texas.

This woman had a sleeping disorder called narcolepsy. Narcolepsy is characterized by episodes of frequent uncontrollable daytime sleeping, usually preceded by drowsiness. The episodes usually occur after meals, but may occur while working or driving a vehicle, having conversation or any sedentary or boring situation.

Prior to my arrival in Corsicana, I was unaware of the council woman's condition and had never experienced or come in contact with someone who had narcolepsy. Actually, I had never even heard of this sleeping disorder.

While I don't have a sleeping disorder, occasionally when I start laughing, I will laugh so hard I might even double over in pain or feel that I am going to have a heart attack. Sometimes I'll need to lie down to stop laughing. Maybe it is a laughing disorder?

My first day on the job in Corsicana was August 16, 1981. Corsicana has a large City Commission Chamber that seats over 100 people. The Commission Chamber includes a sound amplification system to ensure that the voices of the elected officials are heard by the audience.

My second day on the job included a City Commissioners' meeting. During that meeting the council woman fell asleep. As she was sleeping, she leaned forward and began to snore into the microphone. The snoring reverberated throughout the room.

I was very close to losing my composure and almost started to laugh uncontrollably.

After a short period, she awoke and remained awake for the remainder of the meeting.

The third day on the job in Corsicana, I called a department head meeting. I wanted to know who was in charge of the building.

Our Municipal Services Director sheepishly raised his hand and I immediately advised him that I wanted a switch placed at my seat at the Commissioners' table that would switch on and off the commissioner's microphone.

The switch was installed on the fourth day and remained there through the council woman's long term as a City Commissioner. Any time she would fall asleep, I would turn off her microphone in an effort to ensure that she would not be embarrassed and that I would not begin an uncontrollable laugh. The switch proved to be valuable over the years.

KEY INSIGHT

Technology is a wonderful tool, and it just gets better every year. Handing out iPads to the Council and sending them packets electronically sure beats having the Police Department deliver six inch binders on Friday nights. Saves trees too.

"My City Council is very well informed. They can be critical on just about any subject."

Anonymous City Manager, although often quoted by Michael Willis, former ICMA President and as far as we know, the only City Manager to serve professionally on three continents.

Rational Discourse and Public Facilities Often Do Not Mix (As told by James Thurmond)

While City Manager in southwest Texas it became apparent that the community was going to have to acquire and develop a new landfill. Although not urgent we knew it would take several years to accomplish and began the process.

Over a period of about two years, each time we thought that we had found an acceptable site, we would be chased off by the neighbors even though they might live miles from the potential site.

In Southwest Texas, 25 miles is really close and 10 miles is downright neighborly!

Finally we thought we had a good site with a willing seller, no ground water problems, plenty of natural clay, and the nearest residents (who were renters) a full 5 miles away. The site and the residents were all outside the city limits.

Wanting to be a good neighbor and not surprise the residents, the Mayor scheduled a public hearing at City Hall. He was hoping to have rational discourse with the residents on the proposed landfill site.

We hoped to have a calm, thoughtful hearing with the Mayor explaining the city's perspective and the residents presenting their questions and concerns.

Our engineering consultants drove in so that they could

be available for any technical questions and staff spent quite a bit of time preparing a presentation.

On the day of the meeting we put out cookies and soda and met folks as they came in. West Texans are neighborly and the meeting progressed in a civilized manner as long as the Mayor and city staff were presenting the City's justification for the site.

As soon as they finished, and it was time for audience comments, about 30 people in the back of the Council Chamber stood up and held up posters with "NO LANDFILL!" on them and then chanted in loud voices, "No landfill! No landfill! No landfill!"

The meeting was out of control and nothing else rational was said about the landfill.

Once the meeting was adjourned folks stayed to visit and finish the cookies and soda and talk about the weather. The landfill issue was dead for the day and folks were neighborly once again.

We learned from the meeting that even with friendly folks, landfills and rational public discourse do not mix. Simply put, with landfill sites, as with other public facilities such as wastewater treatment plants, jails, wastewater lift stations, and large regional parks, "rational public discourse" is an oxymoron, much like "idle gossip," "small wonder," or "fairly nasty."

This is probably a good example of why direct or pure democracy would not work because either of the following might happen: 1) Public voting would never allow a landfill, wastewater treatment plant, or major public facility to be installed anywhere, or, 2) the public voting would victimize the area or location not having enough votes to prevent the placement of such a facility.

Being an elected official in such a quandary is difficult

and in small or rural communities it can have lasting consequences on relationships.

"I have a theory about trees. The more trees there are the more folks can hide behind them. In West Texas we have very few trees, so folks out here are more open."

Kyle McCain
City Manager

I Won't Ever Ask You to Do Something I Won't Do Myself (As told by "Downtown" Gary Brown)

After becoming City Manager, I got all the employees together and told them that I would not ask them to do a job that I would not do myself. This was in mid-August and during the following winter I was reminded about this statement.

Our surface water plant had some difficulties during a snowstorm and we needed to get our wells ready to pump water. These wells had not been used for a number of years and were going to take some time and effort to get ready.

At one of the wells, we were unable to get the cut-off wrench on the valve so we could pump the water out onto the ground. Upon further observance, the guys could see a decomposing skunk covering the valve. It was determined that the only way to get the skunk out of the way was for someone to lay in the snow and reach in and remove the critter a piece at a time.

After looking at the men who were there at the scene, the statement about "not asking a man to do a job I would not do" was brought up.

To keep my word, I took on the job. It was cold, it was miserable, and although close to losing my lunch on a couple of occasions I knew my credibility was on the line.

Once the work was done, I started toward the pickup of the department supervisor.

When he realized that I was about to open the door and get in, he reached across the seat and locked the door.

He then motioned for me to get in the back and he would take me back to town.

This was a trip of about two miles and the temperature was near 25 degrees.

When we got back to the warehouse, I moved close to the heater and the aroma began to get good. In a very short time I had the stove and warehouse to myself. The rest of the crew was not tough enough to stand the test.

I will say that by doing this, I earned a lot of respect from all our employees.

Town Water (The Smell of Skunk)

Snow on the ground, the weather is cold,
"Start your wells," we were told.
The water you buy may not flow,
To cover the pumps we did not know.
Out to the well field the crew went with haste;
There was no time which we could waste.
The wells hadn't been used for years and years,
What won't work? Brought on the fears.
Replace the fuses, then the breakers close;
I see my breath coming from my nose.
Electricity is flowing, will the pumps pump?
In the superintendent's throat there is a lump.
Out in the open there's not much heat;
To get the water flowing will be a big feat.
Are the valves open or closed? No one knows;
I think there's frost on the end of my nose.
Something is covering the valve on well number five;

We are wondering, "Is it dead or alive?"
Can't see much; the light is dim;
The opening of the pipe is very slim.
There is quite an odor and it's not good;
Nothing near the smell of burning cedar wood.
Covering the valve is a skunk, there is no doubt;
Someone will need to volunteer to get it out.
Colder it seems, the temperature no one knows;
I'm sure, frozen off is the end of my nose!
Recalling part of a speech I had once made;
"Remove the critter," the superintendent did bade.
I would never ask an employee to do a job
    I wouldn't do;
Never walk the walk without a shoe.
This is what the employees remembered best;
Now they would put me to the test.
I lay in the snow and began the task;
As for sympathy, no reason to ask.
The critter was removed a piece at a time;
What was happening to me was a real crime.
The smell of skunk was collecting on me;
Oh, what an odor I soon would be!
The last piece removed, it was time to go;
I got up and brushed off the snow.
Get out of the cold for the trip back to town;
To the superintendent's face did bring a frown.
He had no plans for me to ride
Inside his pickup, he would have rather died.
"Due to your odor you can ride in the back,"
On his face a small grin began to crack.
Frozen! I was a ways past that!
As I crawled in the back and pulled down my hat.
We got back to town; I was as stiff as a board;

Could have gone faster if he'd had a Ford.
I walked into the shop to warm by the fire;
Some new employees I might need to hire...
As I warmed, the odor did too;
All in my clothes and in my shoe.
The next thing I knew I was all alone;
All the employees had up and gone!

KEY INSIGHT

Employees want to be acknowledged for who they are as much as for what they know and can do. Managers do themselves and their folks a great service when they get "out with the troops." The old adage, "Your people do not care how much you know until they know how much you care – about them" continues to be true, especially in local government.

"You can buy people's time; you can buy their physical presence at a given place; you can even buy a measured number of muscular motions per hour. But you cannot buy enthusiasm...you cannot buy loyalty...you cannot buy the devotion of their hearts. This you must earn."

Clarence Francis
Business Executive and Food Expert

The Royal Princess
(As told by Ron Stephens)

There was a lady in one of my communities who dressed like, carried her purse like, and tried to imitate Queen Elizabeth as best she could. She wanted everyone to recognize her as royalty.

She even had the title of "Royal Princess" along with her name printed on her checks.

The women taking water bill payments up front were having difficulty in convincing this lady that she needed to pay her water bill.

Being "of royalty" did not make her exempt from paying her water bill as she thought she ought to be.

She ended up in my office explaining to me that she was royalty and she didn't think that royalty had to pay water bills.

I thought for a minute and then said to her, "Do you have to pay your electric bill and your gas bill?"

She replied, "Yes, they make me pay. They shouldn't, but they do make me pay."

"Well, they make me pay mine, too." I said.

At which time she asked, "Mr. Stephens, are you royalty?"

I said, "Well, my mother thinks I am."

She immediately got up, thanked me, went outside, and paid her water bill.

From that point on, she has paid her bill in a timely manner with never a question asked.

KEY INSIGHT

Being gentle is not the same as being weak. Rick Rigsby, the contemporary motivational speaker, when speaking to the annual conference of TCMA gave this definition of gentleness: "strength under control." The City Manager often has the position, the knowledge and the organizational support structure to be heavy handed or over bearing. Consciously choosing to be gentle is a strength.

"Every person must decide whether to walk in the light of creative altruism or the darkness of destructive selfishness. Life's most persistent and urgent question is, 'What are you doing for others?'"

Martin Luther King, Jr.

Taking the County's Verbal Beating (As told by James Thurmond)

While I was serving as City Manager in a small rural city, a developer proposed to construct apartments outside the city limits next to an exclusive subdivision with very high end homes.

The developer requested water and wastewater collection from the City, and since the apartments did not conflict with the City's Master Plan, and because the County Commissioners' Court had endorsed the apartments, the City Council agreed to provide the utilities.

The residents in the subdivision were outraged, particularly with the County who was doing nothing to stop the apartments. So, the residents scheduled a neighborhood meeting at the Holiday Inn to talk to the County officials and to discuss courses of action.

The Mayor and I thought that it might prove beneficial to attend the meeting but to take a low profile and only listen to the discussion between the County officials and the residents.

We walked into the meeting room at the Holiday Inn, trying not to draw attention to ourselves. We quietly made our way to the back of the room and sat at the rear row of tables so that we would be inconspicuous.

I thought to myself, "This ought to be easy. We are here and basically no one knows it. All we have to do is sit and listen to the County Officials take a verbal beating from the residents."

Gosh, was I surprised when the leader of the residents happened to be sitting at the table next to ours and decided that he would preside over the meeting from his table.

In other words, instead of the Mayor and me sitting at the back of the room, we were now sitting in front of everyone.

Now the rear of the room was the focal point for the meeting.

To add anger to surprise was the fact that none of the County Commissioners or the County Judge showed up for the meeting. The Mayor and I ended up taking the verbal beating that day for a project which was located outside the city limits and which the County had endorsed. We received the blame for the apartments.

KEY INSIGHT

As this story goes to show, there is no poetic justice for cities when dealing with county government. The County was supposed to be on the hot seat because they made a decision which people did not like, but the city took the heat and the county never suffered any consequences. It also goes to show that in a Representative Democracy the governmental officials getting hit over the head may be innocent bystanders, in the wrong place at the wrong time, with the best intentions in the world.

"Be more concerned with your character than with your reputation, because your character is what you really are, while your reputation is merely what others think you are."

John Wooden
Coach

That New City Manager
(As told by Blaine Hinds)

It was only my second week in my new community, and as I arrived at City Hall just a little after 8:00 o'clock, I found a Care Flight helicopter in the middle of the street with several police cars surrounding it.

Lights were flashing everywhere.

I quickly found the incident command center and got a briefing.

It seems that a mental patient had gone berserk, smashing up the dispatch area and several parked police cars with a tire iron.

He then attacked a police officer who was forced to shoot him; fortunately as it turned out, not fatally.

Since there were several citizens standing about I asked one of them if he knew the man.

"Yes," was the answer.

I then asked if he knew what the man's problem was.

He replied, "I think he was looking for that new City Manager."

KEY INSIGHT

In real estate the old saying is that the three most important things are location, location and location. In city
management the three most important things often are
timing, timing and timing.

It is a lot more fun to manage a community on the rise,
so catching a favorable economic tide or a series of good
elected officials can make a big difference.

As Blaine found out, sometimes being just a few minutes
late can also make a big difference.

"I used to think running an organization was equivalent to
conducting a symphony orchestra. But I don't think that is
quite it; it's more like jazz. There is more improvisation."

Warren Bennis
Management Consultant

Tight Lipped
(A totally fabricated fable as told about Virgil Basgall by his many friends and admirers to demonstrate both his resolve and frugality.)

As the new City Manager in Hays, KS in the late 1940's Virgil and his wife, Winnie, were invited as dignitaries to the local county fair – a big deal in Western Kansas.

Virgil was notoriously frugal with money (his as well as the city's) and for most of his life rarely carried more than ten dollars at any one time in his pocket.

Because of the War, air flight and planes had come a long way, and while at the fair they were approached by a "barn stormer" who offered to take Virgil for a ride for just ten dollars.

Virgil declined, saying, "Ten dollars is ten dollars only as long as it is in my pocket."

After much dickering the pilot finally made an offer Virgil couldn't turn down.

"I tell you what," the pilot said, "I will take you both up, and if you can ride with me without saying a word the ride will be free."

Since Virgil was as tight lipped as he was frugal he

agreed to the deal.

Sure enough it was an incredible ride with many loops and stalls and treetop thrills – not that there were many trees in Western Kansas at the time.

Finally, the pilot gave up on getting a scream or holler out of Virgil and landed the plane.

Upon completing his taxi and shutting down his engine he was shocked to see that only Winnie was left.

"Where is Virgil?" the pilot exclaimed breathlessly.

"Ohh, he fell out some time ago."

"Why didn't you say anything?" the pilot demanded.

"Ohh, well, Virgil always says, ten dollars is only ten dollars as long as it is in his pocket, and I knew he would be very upset if I had said a word."

PS. When I asked Virgil about this story many years ago he said: "Never happened, but I would have been proud of Winnie if it had."

PPS. Virgil passed in July 2009 at the age of 97. Both KACM and Emporia State University have scholarhips in his name. For more than ten dollars.

> **KEY INSIGHT**
> Virgil was one of the last of the breed of the early City Managers. As reformers for local government they lived out the credo, "Without Fear or Favor." His influence continues, much like a multi-level marketing scheme, and the list of the City Managers who worked for Virgil reads like a who's who.

"Virgil was one of the worst golfers to ever play the game, and nobody loved the game more. Hosting the tournament named in his honor was the highlight of his year and I think getting ready for it helped him become active every spring, keeping him young well into his nineties."

Stan Stewart
Former City Manager and
Virgil's long-time KACM golf partner

Look Them In the Eye
(As told by Mike Conduff)

I almost didn't get to work with Marvelous Marvin Tate.
The newspaper in Bryan, TX where Marvin was Mayor found out about me being offered the City Manager's job there and called the newspaper in Manhattan, KS where I was working at the time. The Editor of the Manhattan Mercury called my Mayor for a comment and things got public and crazy from there.

The Mayor, whom I really liked and out of courtesy had told that I had a job offer and was seriously considering it, used the resulting newspaper coverage about my potential leaving to try to leverage a "stay here" package. My supporters in the business and university communities urged the Mayor to pull out all the stops, and to his credit he did as much as he could reasonably be expected to do for the time and place.

Being told you are wanted is a siren song for a City Manager and after a called emergency session of the Manhattan City Commission, I had made up my mind that I would indeed stay in Manhattan. Our family enjoyed the community very much and we had made friendships there that last today. The President of Kansas State University called urging me to stay, and even the editorial board of the Mercury got in the act and wrote an almost unprecedented editorial encouraging me to think about all the good I could do for K-State and the Little Apple if I remained in place.

So, having made up my mind to stay, and following the long standing ethical tradition of calling the courting community to let them know, I got Marvin on the phone. I walked him though the situation and told him that I had made up my mind to stay, but wanted to give him a personal courtesy call.

A bit about Marvin will help the rest of the story.

Marvin was a Junction Boy. It took me several years of working and living in the shadow of Texas A&M University in Bryan+College Station to fully appreciate that legacy. When Marvin was in college at TAMU he was a star football player and in 1954, the year he was a senior (and I was born) Paul "Bear" Bryant came to town as coach. One of The Bear's first actions was to take the entire football team to Junction, TX to practice before the season.

If you have seen the movie or read the book you know it was brutal. Marvin and his team mates practiced 12 hours a day in 110 degree plus heat with little or no water. Over 100 players began the endeavor, only 35 survived it. Suffice it to quote Marvin, "We went out on three buses and came back on one – and it wasn't full."

After playing for Bear Bryant, Marvin went on to a great career and became Athletic Director at A&M, a position he held for many years.

In this role Marvin had recruited and hired many head coaches. As they say in Texas, "This was not his first rodeo."

While I was laying out all of my reasons for staying in Manhattan, Marvin remained largely silent. When I was done he agreed that it made sense financially for me to stay where I was.

Then he said, "Mike, let me ask you a question. I know we recruited you for this position, but why did you decide to apply for this job?"

Now, he knew the answer to the question as I had told him and the full council that as part of the interview. Further I knew he knew, and he knew I knew he knew. But, out of courtesy I answered again. Bigger community, bigger state, the opportunity to work with a popular directly elected mayor, increased stability with more opportunity, etc., etc.

He then asked, "Has any of that changed?"

I had to answer truthfully, "No, Marvin."

He went on. "Mike, let me ask you another question. If they love you so much there in Manhattan, why did it take you leaving for them to offer you additional money and benefits?"

I considered that a rhetorical question, so didn't answer, but didn't really have to. He knew he had scored a key point and taken a lot of the wind out of my sails.

Then he went for the jugular. "Mike, you and I would make a great team. I have lots I want to do here. Why don't you get off that dead back end of yours and come down and go to work with me?"

What could I say to that but "gig 'em!"

So we packed up and came to Bryan. Working with Marvin was all I thought it would be. He knew his role to a tee and he supported me in all I did. I never once worried about my back because I knew Marvin had it. He knew everyone, had incredible connections, not the least of which was the Aggie network, and could tell more stories than anyone I had ever met. He was so polished he would meet someone once and the next time he saw them, he could call them by name and would remember where they went to college.

I hadn't been in town long enough for the Kansas dust to wash off my LTD when Marvin took me to lunch with the President of Blinn College. Over lunch Marvin and the President laid out their vision for a unified central campus that would act both as a matriculation facility for the enrollment capped A&M and as a stand-alone educational facility for those students who wanted employable skills and training.

With my marching orders in hand we went to work. Land availability, infrastructure, access, zoning, financing. Everything was researched and vetted, and ultimately the location, mechanisms and time line were established. This was going to be a three run homer if not a grand slam for the community. Marvin and the Council were ecstatic.

Then it got ugly. The neighborhood (across a four lane arterial roadway) led by only a couple of short-term residents got vocal about taking this sizeable piece of overgrown, mosquito infested, virtually abandoned property – "green space" they called it – and converting it to a college. "The reason," they said, "we bought our houses here was because of the soothing effects of this space."

Never mind that it was privately owned. Never mind that they had complained nonstop about skunks, rats and snakes invading their neighborhood because of the neglect of this property. Never mind that it had been listed with a realtor for months. Never mind that the community college use was way less intensive than zoning allowed. Never mind. When folks are being whipped up facts don't matter and reason rarely prevails.

It got so hostile that supporters started dropping like flies. There is nothing like an angry neighborhood to suck up scarce resources. It wasn't long before the City was squarely in the crosshairs and I was beginning to feel like I had a target on my chest.

Fortunately Marvin had been to Junction, and nothing

he ever faced subsequently held much fear for him. "After you have had your butt chewed out by Coach Bryant, there isn't enough left for anyone else to get a hold of," he would say.

He also had great insight in working with people. "Mike, you have been allowing this handful of folks to control the process. There are many great people in that neighborhood, what you need to do is figure out how to reach them and get them engaged."

So with Marvin's direction we set up a neighborhood dessert social, in the neighborhood, at their local elementary school.

Knowing that the "silent majority" would not otherwise attend we sent out personal invitations over Marvin's hand written signature (he penned personal notes on most of them.) We had homemade desserts, a very enjoyable mingling time and ultimately the equivalent of a fireside chat in the cafeteria.

Marvin sat up front and after a few short presentations, complete with gorgeous artist's renderings of the proposed campus, stood up and gave the equivalent of Knute Rockney's "Win one for The Gipper" speech.

I was thinking to myself, "Wow, Marvelous is on his game tonight! These folks are likely to head over to the site right now and start using shovels to help us."

When Marvin got done I expected a standing ovation for him.

Instead, in one of the great shocks of my career, one of the folks in the front row began to boo my incredible mayor. A boo. Loud, obnoxious and affronting. A boo like you might hear from the Longhorns when the Texas A&M Aggies took the field in Austin.

I simply did not know what to do. A boo was totally

out of character for Bryan+College Station. You see, Aggies don't boo. Part of their great tradition is sportsmanship. They might "hiss" and they even have an Aggie Yell they use when a ref blows a call; "Riffity riffity riff-raff, chiffity chiffity chiff-chaff, riff-raff, chiff-chaff, let's give the ref a horse laugh, ssss." But they never boo.

If the booer would have stood up and slapped Marvin I would not have been more shocked.

I admired Marvin so much I was ready to tackle this booer myself, and was just waiting for Marvin to tear him to pieces.

Instead Marvelous just stood there and took it. He looked the booer right in the eye and took it.

Then he said, "I guess that means you don't like the project," and smiled that warm friendly gotta love me smile of his, and the rest of the crowd just started laughing. At first it was just a shocked reaction laugh, but as the crowd thought about it, it became a genuine, responsive enjoyable laugh.

When the chuckles died down, one of the long-time and highly respected neighbors stood up on his own and said, "We are all friends and neighbors here, let's remember that tonight."

The booer did not say another word the whole evening and never had any clout again. He didn't quit fighting the project and he never did like us even a little, but he never again was able to marshal any support.

The next day I met Marvin in his office to tell him how impressed I was with how he handled himself and to thank him for being willing to take the point.

I will never forget his words, or the lesson.

Marvin said, "Mike, at the end of the day you have got to go look them in the eye. It's not always fun and sometimes it doesn't turn out like you want, but you have got to get up close and personal."

And then, being Marvin, he told a Coach Bryant story. "When we were in Junction, and so many of the players had already left or been carried off the field, Coach Bryant got us together and he said, 'Boys, give me your best. Play for me. I promise I will put you through hell, but in the end, we'll be champions.' He did and we were."

Postscript:

Today Blinn College in Bryan is a model institution. It's 10,000 plus enrollment makes it an economic engine for the entire region. Coupled with Texas A&M, just minutes away, higher education remains the foundation for the communities. Marvin's vision was a great one.

KEY INSIGHT

The willingness to meet people where they are is a key success factor for local government leaders. Boxer Joe Louis is quoted as saying, "You can run, but you can't hide," and nowhere is that more true than in local government. Angry crowds can sense fear. If you will take the time to understand their issues, look them in the eye and have a civil discourse much can be accomplished.

Bear Bryant, (all used by Marvelous Marvin Tate)
"Never quit. It is the easiest cop-out in the world. Set a goal and don't quit until you attain it. When you do attain it, set another goal, and don't quit until you reach it. Never quit."
"It's not the will to win, but the will to prepare to win that makes the difference."
"In life, you'll have your back up against the wall many times. You might as well get used to it."
"If you believe in yourself and have dedication and pride - and never quit, you'll be a winner. The price of victory is high but so are the rewards."
"If anything goes bad, I did it. If anything goes semi-good, we did it. If anything goes really good, then you did it. That's all it takes to get people to win football games for you."
And Marvin's favorite:
"In a crisis, don't hide behind anything or anybody. They're going to find you anyway."

ICMA Code of Ethics

With Guidelines

The ICMA Code of Ethics was adopted by the ICMA membership in 1924, and most recently amended by the membership in May 1998. The Guidelines for the Code were adopted by the ICMA Executive Board in 1972, and most recently revised in July 2004.

The mission of ICMA is to create excellence in local governance by developing and fostering professional local government management worldwide. To further this mission, certain principles, as enforced by the Rules of Procedure, shall govern the conduct of every member of ICMA, who shall:

-

1. Be dedicated to the concepts of effective and democratic local government by responsible elected officials and believe that professional general management is essential to the achievement of this objective.

2. Affirm the dignity and worth of the services rendered by government and maintain a constructive, creative, and practical attitude toward local government affairs and a deep sense of social responsibility as a trusted public servant.

Advice to Officials of Other Local Governments. When members advise and respond to inquiries from elected or appointed officials of other local governments, they should inform the administrators of those communities.

3. Be dedicated to the highest ideals of honor and integrity in all public and personal relationships in order that the member may merit the respect and confidence of the elected officials, of other officials and employees, and of the public.

Public Confidence. Members should conduct themselves so as to maintain public confidence in their profession, their local government, and in their performance of the public trust.

Impression of Influence. Members should conduct their official and personal affairs in such a manner as to give the clear impression that they cannot be improperly influenced in the performance of their official duties.

Appointment Commitment. Members who accept an appointment to a position should not fail to report for that position. This does not preclude the possibility of a member considering several offers or seeking several positions at the same time, but once a *bona fide* offer of a position has been accepted, that commitment should be honored. Oral acceptance of an employment offer is considered binding unless the employer makes fundamental changes in terms of employment.

Credentials. An application for employment or for ICMA's Voluntary Credentialing Program should be complete and accurate as to all pertinent details of education, experience, and personal history. Members should recognize that both omissions and inaccuracies must be avoided.

Professional Respect. Members seeking a management position should show professional respect for persons formerly holding the position or for others who might be applying for the same position. Professional respect does not preclude honest differences of opinion; it does preclude attacking a person's motives or integrity in order to be appointed to a position.

Reporting Ethics Violations. When becoming aware of a possible violation of the ICMA Code of Ethics, members are encouraged to report the matter to ICMA. In reporting the matter, members may choose to go on record as the complainant or report the matter on a confidential basis.

Confidentiality. Members should not discuss or divulge information with anyone about pending or completed ethics cases, except as specifically authorized by the Rules of Procedure for Enforcement of the Code of Ethics.

Seeking Employment. Members should not seek employment for a position having an incumbent administrator who has not resigned or been officially informed that his or her services are to be terminated.

4. Recognize that the chief function of local government at all times is to serve the best interests of all of the people.

Length of Service. A minimum of two years generally is considered necessary in order to render a professional service to the local government. A short tenure should be the exception rather than a recurring experience. However, under special circumstances, it may be in the best interests of the local government and the member to separate in a shorter time. Examples of such circumstances would include refusal of the appointing authority to honor commitments concerning conditions of employment, a vote of no confidence in the member, or severe personal problems. It is the responsibility of an applicant for a position to ascertain conditions of employment. Inadequately determining terms of employment prior to arrival does not justify premature termination.

5. Submit policy proposals to elected officials; provide them with facts and advice on matters of policy as a basis for making decisions and setting community goals; and uphold and implement local government policies adopted by elected officials.

Conflicting Roles. Members who serve multiple roles--working as both city attorney and city manager for the same community, for example--should avoid participating in matters that create the appearance of a conflict of interest. They should disclose the potential conflict to the governing body so that other opinions may be solicited.

6. Recognize that elected representatives of the people are entitled to the credit for the establishment of local government policies; responsibility for policy execution rests with the members.

7. Refrain from all political activities which undermine public confidence in professional administrators. Refrain from participation in the election of the members of the employing legislative body.

Elections of the Governing Body. Members should maintain a reputation for serving equally and impartially all members of the governing body of the local government they serve, regardless of party. To this end, they should not engage in active participation in the election campaign on behalf of or in opposition to candidates for the governing body.

Elections of Elected Executives. Members should not engage in the election campaign of any candidate for mayor or elected county executive.

Running for Office. Members shall not run for elected office or become involved in political activities related to running for elected office. They shall not seek political endorsements, financial contributions or engage in other campaign activities.

Elections. Members share with their fellow citizens the right and responsibility to vote and to voice their opinion on public issues. However, in order not to impair their effectiveness on behalf of the local governments they serve, they shall not participate in political activities to support the candidacy of individuals running for any city, county, special district, school, state or federal offices. Specifically, they shall not endorse candidates, make financial contributions, sign or circulate petitions, or participate in fund-raising activities for individuals seeking or holding elected office.

Elections on the Council-Manager Plan. Members may assist in preparing and presenting materials that explain the council-manager form of government to the public prior to an election on the use of the plan. If assistance is required by another community, members may respond. All activities regarding ballot issues should be conducted within local regulations and in a professional manner.

Presentation of Issues. Members may assist the governing body in presenting issues involved in referenda such as bond issues, annexations, and similar matters.

8. Make it a duty continually to improve the member's professional ability and to develop the competence of associates in the use of management techniques.

Self-Assessment. Each member should assess his or her professional skills and abilities on a periodic basis.

Professional Development. Each member should commit at least 40 hours per year to professional development activities that are based on the practices identified by the members of ICMA.

9. Keep the community informed on local government affairs; encourage communication between the citizens and

all local government officers; emphasize friendly and courteous service to the public; and seek to improve the quality and image of public service.

10. Resist any encroachment on professional responsibilities, believing the member should be free to carry out official policies without interference, and handle each problem without discrimination on the basis of principle and justice.

Information Sharing. The member should openly share information with the governing body while diligently carrying out the member's responsibilities as set forth in the charter or enabling legislation.

11. Handle all matters of personnel on the basis of merit so that fairness and impartiality govern a member's decisions pertaining to appointments, pay adjustments, promotions, and discipline.

Equal Opportunity. All decisions pertaining to appointments, pay adjustments, promotions, and discipline should prohibit discrimination because of race, color, religion, sex, national origin, sexual orientation, political affiliation, disability, age, or marital status.

It should be the members' personal and professional responsibility to actively recruit and hire a diverse staff throughout their organizations.

12. Seek no favor; believe that personal aggrandizement or profit secured by confidential information or by misuse of public time is dishonest.

Gifts. Members should not directly or indirectly solicit any gift or accept or receive any gift--whether it be money, services, loan, travel, entertainment, hospitality, promise, or any other form--under the following circumstances: (1) it could be reasonably inferred or expected that the gift was intended to influence them in the performance of their official duties; or (2) the gift was intended to serve as a reward for any official action on their part.

It is important that the prohibition of unsolicited gifts be limited to circumstances related to improper influence. In *de minimus* situations, such as meal checks, some modest maximum dollar value should be determined by the member as a guideline. The guideline is not intended to isolate members from normal social practices where gifts among friends, associates, and relatives are appropriate for certain occasions.

Investments in Conflict with Official Duties. Member should not invest or hold any investment, directly or indirectly, in any financial business, commercial, or other private transaction that creates a conflict with their official duties.

In the case of real estate, the potential use of confidential information and knowledge to further a member's personal interest requires special consideration. This guideline recognizes that members' official actions and decisions can be influenced if there is a conflict with personal investments. Purchases and sales which might be interpreted as speculation for quick profit ought to be avoided (see the guideline on "Confidential Information").

Because personal investments may prejudice or may appear to influence official actions and decisions, members may, in concert with their governing body, provide for disclosure of such investments prior to accepting their position as local government administrator or prior to any official action by the governing body that may affect such investments.

Personal Relationships. Members should disclose any personal relationship to the governing body in any instance where there could be the appearance of a conflict of interest. For example, if the manager's spouse works for a developer doing business with the local government, that fact should be disclosed.

Confidential Information. Members should not disclose to others, or use to further their personal interest, confidential information acquired by them in the course of their official duties.

Private Employment. Members should not engage in, solicit, negotiate for, or promise to accept private employment, nor should they render services for private interests or conduct a private business when such employment, service, or business creates a conflict with or impairs the proper discharge of their official duties.

Teaching, lecturing, writing, or consulting are typical activities that may not involve conflict of interest, or impair the proper discharge of their official duties. Prior notification of the appointing authority is appropriate in all cases of outside employment.

Representation. Members should not represent any outside interest before any agency, whether public or private, except with the authorization of or at the direction of the appointing authority they serve.

Endorsements. Members should not endorse commercial products or services by agreeing to use their photograph, endorsement, or quotation in paid or other commercial advertisements, whether or not for compensation. Members may, however, agree to endorse the following, provided they do not receive any compensation: (1) books or other publications; (2) professional development or educational services provided by nonprofit membership organizations or recognized educational institutions; (3) products and/or services in which the local government has a direct economic interest.

Members' observations, opinions, and analyses of commercial products used or tested by their local governments are appropriate and useful to the profession when included as part of professional articles and reports.

ICMA Code of Ethics:

Rules of Procedure for Enforcement

Adopted by the ICMA Executive Board and revised in September 2005

I. General

A. These rules govern the procedures for enforcing the ICMA Code of Ethics as adopted by the ICMA membership.

B. All members of ICMA agree to abide by the Code of Ethics.

C. The purpose of these rules is to provide a reasonable process for investigating and determining whether a member has violated the code, and to afford each individual member who is the subject of an investigation (the "respondent") a full and fair opportunity to be heard throughout the process.

D. It is the intention of the ICMA membership that these rules be carried out carefully but expeditiously in order to minimize the time during which a member may be subject to possible disciplinary action. Accordingly, time limits stated in these rules are binding, subject to extensions which may be granted by the Committee on Professional Conduct (CPC), or the ICMA executive director, for reasonable cause, upon request.

E. No person may participate in any proceedings on a complaint brought under these rules if that person is or may be a witness or complainant in that case, or if his or her participation would otherwise create, or appear to create, a conflict of interest. The executive director may select a replacement for any person (other than a member of the Executive Board) who is unable to participate in the case for this reason.

II. Jurisdiction

A. All members of ICMA in active service to a local government are subject to the Code of Ethics and are subject to sanctions for any violations thereof which occur during their membership. However, elected officials are not subject to Tenet 7, and members not in service are subject only to Tenets 1 and 3. A member may be subject to sanctions for a violation which continues while he or she is a member even though the conduct in question originated prior to admission to membership.

B. If a complaint is made against a person who was a member at the time the alleged violation occurred, but who is not a member at the time the complaint is made, the complaint will be processed under these procedures only if the former member agrees in writing. In no event shall a person be readmitted to membership if there is an outstanding and unresolved complaint against him or her for conduct while formerly a member.

C. The committee shall retain jurisdiction over an investigation of a respondent who, before the conclusion of the investigation, resigns from ICMA or otherwise allows his or her membership in ICMA to lapse.

III. Responsibilities

A. The ICMA Executive Board is responsible for making the final decision on matters pertaining to the enforcement of the code, including, but not limited to, sanctions for the violation thereof. No current or former member may be publicly censured, expelled, or barred from membership without the approval of the Executive Board.

B. The Committee on Professional Conduct (CPC) is the committee of ICMA responsible for assisting the Executive Board in implementing these rules and has the specific duties set forth hereinafter.

   1. The CPC shall consist of three or more members of the ICMA Executive Board who shall be selected by the president of ICMA.

   2. CPC members shall serve for terms of one (1) year or until their successors are chosen by the president.

C. A state association consists of members of ICMA within the particular state or province. It is responsible for appointing fact-finding committees.

D. A fact-finding committee is a committee of ICMA, appointed by a state association, and is responsible for conducting the investigation of a complaint of a violation of the code in accordance with these rules. Members of a fact-finding committee shall serve until the conclusion of the investigation they were appointed to conduct, or until such later date as the state association of ICMA members may request.

E. The executive director shall assist the Executive Board and the CPC in enforcing the code and implementing these rules. It is the responsibility of the executive director to publicize the existence and importance of the code with elected officials and the general public.

    1. The executive director may privately advise members on the ethical implications of their conduct under the code. However, the opinion or advice of the executive director shall not be binding on the Executive Board, the CPC, or any fact-finding committee.

    2. The executive director may designate a member of the ICMA staff to carry out any of the responsibilities assigned to the executive director under these rules.

IV. Sanctions

A. Sanctions may be imposed in accordance with these rules upon members who are found to have violated the code. In determining the kind of sanction to be imposed, the following factors may be considered: the nature of the violation, prior violations by the same individual, the willfulness of the violation, the level of professional or public responsibility of the individual, and any other factors which bear upon the seriousness of the violation.

B. The following sanctions may be imposed singly or in combination at the conclusion of an investigation and/or hearing under these rules:

1. Private Censure. A letter to the respondent, the state association, and the complainant, indicating that the respondent has been found to have violated the Code of Ethics, that ICMA disapproves of such conduct, and that, if it is repeated in the future, it may be cause for more serious sanctions. If the complainant is a nonmember, he or she shall be notified that the case was considered and resolved, and that no public action was taken.

2. Public Censure. Notification to the respondent, complainant, state association, and news media, indicating that a violation of the code took place and that ICMA strongly disapproves of such conduct and the nature of the sanction(s) imposed. In addition, such notice shall be provided to appropriate local governing bodies where the Executive Board has found it necessary to do so in order to protect the public against unethical conduct in local government.

3. Expulsion. A revocation of the respondent's membership privileges.

4. Membership Bar. A prohibition against reinstatement of the respondent's membership in ICMA.

C. Upon receiving documented evidence that a member

has been found guilty after trial by a judge or a jury of criminal conduct, which constitutes a violation of the ICMA Code of Ethics and which occurred while the person was a member of ICMA, the executive director shall immediately issue a notice of suspension of membership to that person by registered mail and that person's membership shall be suspended as of the date of that notice. The executive director shall advise the CPC of any such action and shall refer the case to the CPC. The CPC may commence an investigation in accordance with Part VI hereof, or it may defer proceedings until the person has exhausted all appeals or the time for appeal has expired. The suspension shall continue in effect until such time as sanctions provided under Part IV.B. are imposed, or the case is dismissed, in accordance with these Rules.

D. A member who has been barred or expelled from membership under these rules may apply for reinstatement to ICMA membership only after a period of at least five (5) years from the date of the bar or expulsion, or from the date of the last review of a request for reinstatement. The barred or expelled former member must submit a written request to the Executive Board for a reinstatement review and include the reasons why he or she believes it should be considered. Such requests shall automatically be referred to the CPC. The CPC may ask state associations to provide additional information through a fact-finding process. The CPC will review all the information provided, including any state association reports, and make a recommendation to the Executive Board. The former member requesting reinstatement review is entitled to a hearing before the Executive Board.

V. Initiation of Procedures

A. Proceedings against an individual for an alleged violation of the Code of Ethics may be initiated by the executive director upon receiving a written complaint or other written information from any source indicating that a violation may have occurred.

B. Upon receiving such a written complaint or information, the executive director must ascertain whether it is sufficiently clear and complete to initiate proceedings, and, if so, whether it alleges conduct that may be a violation of the Code of Ethics. If the executive director concludes that the complaint is not sufficiently clear or complete to initiate proceedings, he or she shall seek further clarification from the complainant or other source before taking any further action.

   1. If the executive director cannot determine whether the conduct alleged, if proven, might violate the Code of Ethics, he or she shall refer the question to the CPC for a ruling. No further action shall be taken with respect to the complaint or information unless the CPC rules that the conduct alleged, if true, may constitute a violation of the code.

   2. If the executive director concludes that the complaint is sufficiently clear and complete to initiate proceedings, and may, if proven, indicate a violation of the code, a copy of the complaint or information shall be forwarded

by registered mail to the respondent named in the complaint or information. The respondent shall be informed at the time of the provisions of the code which he or she is alleged to have violated. The executive director may also request that the respondent answer specific questions pertaining to the alleged violation.

3. The respondent shall be given thirty (30) days within which to respond in writing to the complaint or information, to provide any further information or material he or she considers relevant to the allegations, and to answer any specific questions asked by the executive director.

4. As soon as the respondent's response is received, but in no event more than thirty (30) days after written notice of the alleged violation has been given to the respondent, the executive director shall refer the case to the CPC for proceedings in accordance with these rules.

VI. Investigations

A. Upon receiving a case of an alleged violation of the Code of Ethics from the executive director, the CPC shall commence an investigation into the allegations. However, no investigation shall be required if (1) the respondent admits to the violation in his or her initial response, or (2) the respondent has already entered a guilty plea, or has been found guilty and has exhausted all appeals, in a criminal case involving the same conduct.

B. In all cases other than those in which an investigation is not required, the executive director, at the request of the CPC, shall request the state association for the state in which the violation is alleged to have occurred to appoint an ICMA fact-finding committee to conduct the investigation. If the violation is alleged to have occurred in more than one state, at least one member of the committee shall be from the state involved. In the event that there is no active association in a state, the CPC shall appoint an ICMA fact-finding committee from one or more state(s) for this purpose.

1. The fact-finding committee shall consist of not less than three (3) ICMA members. No one other than an ICMA member may serve on the ICMA fact-finding committee.

2. A fact-finding committee must be appointed within fifteen (15) days of the request made by the executive director.

3. The fact-finding committee shall afford the respondent an opportunity to meet with the committee in person and may, at its discretion, afford such an opportunity to the complainant as well. The respondent may appear at such a meeting personally and be accompanied by a representative. Alternatively, the respondent may appear through a representative.

4. The fact-finding committee shall prepare and maintain notes of all meetings and interviews

with the respondent, the complainant, and any witnesses, and may request any such person to sign a statement prepared on the basis of those notes. The respondent shall be entitled to review these notes and statements, and any other documentary evidence gathered in the course of the investigation, and shall be afforded the opportunity to respond in writing thereto.

5. The fact-finding committee shall take all reasonable steps to ascertain the facts relevant to the case, including, but not limited to, interviews with witnesses, review of the respondent's submission(s), and examination of all published material judged to be relevant and reliable.

6. Within sixty (60) days of the appointment of the fact-finding committee, the investigation shall be concluded, and a written report of the committee's proposed findings of fact shall be sent to the executive director and the respondent. Each finding must be supported by reliable and relevant evidence which has been made available to the respondent for review.

VII. Decisions

A. The CPC shall promptly review the fact-finding committee's proposed findings of fact and shall ascertain whether they are supported by sufficient reliable and relevant evidence.

1. If the evidence is not sufficient, the CPC may

either (a) dismiss the case; (b) return it to the fact-finding committee for further investigation in accordance with these rules; or (c) refer the case to the Executive Board for a hearing in accordance with part VIII of these rules.

2. If the CPC determines that the proposed findings are supported by the evidence, it shall determine whether they demonstrate that a violation of the Code of Ethics has occurred. If not, it shall dismiss the case and so advise the respondent, the fact-finding committee, the state association, and the executive director.

3. If the CPC concludes on the basis of the fact-finding committee's report that a violation has occurred, it shall determine the appropriate sanction(s). The CPC shall then notify the respondent of its intent to adopt the fact-finding committee's report as final, and to impose the specified sanction(s) for the reasons stated, unless the respondent can show that the findings of facts are erroneous, or that the proposed sanctions(s) should not be imposed in light of certain mitigating factors which the CPC did not previously consider. The respondent shall have fifteen (15) days in which to submit a written response to the CPC and/or to request a hearing.

4. In event that the respondent makes no submission, and does not request a hearing, the CPC shall promptly adopt the proposed findings and sanction(s) as final and so inform the

Executive Director.

5. In the event that the respondent makes a written submission, but does not request a hearing, the CPC shall review the submission and may either adopt, or revise and adopt as revised, the proposed findings and/or sanction(s), as it deems appropriate. The CPC shall promptly notify the Executive Director of its decision.

6. In the event that the respondent requests a hearing, the CPC shall refer the case, including its recommended sanction(s), for a hearing before the Executive Board. Hearings shall be conducted in accordance with part VIII of these rules. No sanction(s) shall be imposed before the hearing is concluded.

B. Upon receiving notice from the CPC of its determination that a private censure is the appropriate sanction, and that the respondent has not requested a hearing, the executive director shall send a letter of private censure to the respondent, with copies to the complainant and the state association. The case shall then be closed.

1. No other notification of a private censure shall be made. However, ICMA may publish the fact that certain kinds of conduct have resulted in the issuance of private censures, provided that no names or identifying details are disclosed.

C. Upon receiving notice from the CPC of its determination that a public censure, expulsion, or membership bar is the appropriate sanction, and that the respondent has not requested a hearing, the Executive Board may vote to adopt the recommended decision of the CPC, to modify said decision, or to dismiss the case without imposing sanctions. The respondent shall be immediately notified of the decision of the Executive Board and the sanction, if any, shall be implemented.

VIII. Hearings

A. These procedures shall govern all hearings conducted pursuant to these rules.

B. No board member may hear any case if his or her participation in that case would create an actual or apparent conflict of interest.

C. Within ten (10) days of receiving a request for a hearing, the executive director shall notify the respondent by registered or certified mail that a hearing has been scheduled before the Executive Board. The hearing date shall be at least fifteen (15) days after the date the notice is postmarked. The notice shall also state that the respondent has the following rights:

1. To appear personally at the hearing;

2. To be accompanied and represented at the hearing by an attorney or other representative;

3. To review all documentary evidence, if any, against him or her in advance of the hearing;

4. To cross-examine any witness who testifies against him or her at the hearing; and

5. To submit documentary evidence, and to present testimony, including the respondent's, in his or her defense at the hearing.

D. The Executive Board shall not be bound by any formal rules of evidence but may accord appropriate weight to the evidence based on its relevance and reliability.

1. The fact-finding committee's report shall be admissible evidence at the hearing.

2. The Executive Board may not hear evidence of any alleged ethics violation by the respondent that was not the subject of the initial investigation.

E. At any hearing conducted under these rules, the CPC shall first present evidence in support of its recommended decision. Upon conclusion of its presentation, the respondent shall have the opportunity to present evidence in his or her defense.

F. Within five (5) working days of the conclusion of the hearing, the Executive Board shall render a decision in the case.

1. The decision shall be in writing and shall include a statement of the reasons therefore. Only evidence which was put before the Executive Board may be considered as a basis for the decision.

2. The Executive Board's decision may be to:

a. Dismiss the case;

b. Adopt the findings and sanction(s) recommended by the CPC; or

c. Revise, and adopt as revised, the findings and/or sanction(s) recommended by the CPC. However, the Executive Board may not increase the sanction(s) recommended by the CPC unless new evidence, not previously available to the CPC, is disclosed at the hearing, which indicates that the respondent's violation was more serious. No sanction may be imposed for any violation of which the respondent had no prior notice.

3. A copy of the written decision of the Executive Board shall be sent immediately by registered mail to the respondent, the Executive Board, the CPC, the state association, and the executive director.

4. Promptly after receiving a copy of the written decision, the executive director shall implement the sanction(s), if any, imposed by the Executive Board in accordance with the rules.

IX. Revocation of Credential

The Rules shall also apply to the revocation of a member's credential under the ICMA Credentialing Program, as approved by the ICMA Executive Board.

About the Author

Michael A. (Mike) Conduff is the President and CEO of The Elim Group – *Your Governance Experts*, a governance, leadership, training, speaking and consulting firm. Mike has 35+ years of leadership, management and governance experience, having served as the City Manager of four different University communities, most recently as the City Manager of Denton, Texas. Denton is the home of The University of North Texas and Texas Woman's University. Located in the dynamic North Texas Corridor, Denton is an innovative and rapidly growing community of 125,000. Prior to assuming the City Manager's position in Denton in May 2001, Mike was a nine-year City Manager of Bryan, Texas, a 1998 & 1999 All-America City Finalist and the birthplace of Texas A&M University. Before he came to Texas, Mike served as City Manager in Manhattan, Kansas, home of Kansas State University, for five years. He also served as City Manager of Pittsburg, Kansas, home of Pittsburg State University, for 5½ years where he also served as a line employee and department head.

Mr. Conduff earned his B.S. in civil engineering at the University of New Hampshire, graduating Cum Laude. His M.B.A. is from Pittsburg State University. He is also a charter graduate of the Carver Policy Governance® Academy and is a past Chair of the Board of Directors of the International Policy Governance® Association. Mike's clients have included the International City/County Management Association, The National League of Cities Leadership Training Institute, The National Committee on Planned Giving, The Community Associations Institute, The Republic of the Marshall Islands, and many many cities, counties, associations, and other non-profit and for-profit corporations. In addition to *Democracy at the Doorstep – True Stories from the Green Berets of Public Administrators* he is the co-author of *The OnTarget Board Member – 8 Indisputable Behaviors*, now in its second edition, *Bottom Line Green – How America's Cities are Saving the Planet (And Money Too!)*, and *The Policy Governance® Fieldbook*, a book on the practical applications of Policy Governance®. Additionally he writes a regular column for Public Management Magazine and is frequently featured in other national publications. Known as a "master of motivation," he is a sought after and frequent speaker at international, national, regional and state-wide conferences, seminars and events.

In addition to serving the International City/County Management Association as a Senior Advisor for Governance, Mr. Conduff is a Fellow of the prestigious National Academy of Public Administration. He has been honored with the 2006 TCMA Mentoring Award in memory of Gary Gwyn, the 2004 International Award for Career Development in Memory of L. P. (Perry) Cookingham from ICMA, and the especially meaningful Joy Sansom Mentor Award from the Urban Management Assistants of North Texas for his commitment to helping others achieve their potential. The Center for Digital Government has awarded Mike their coveted "Best of Texas 2004 Visionary Award."

A fifth generation Native American, Mike grew up on stories of his Cherokee ancestry, and attributes his love of motivational speaking and telling stories to his grandmothers. A graduate of the 1988 Leadership Kansas Class, Mr. Conduff is active in a number of professional and civic organizations. He serves on the Athletic Council for the University of North Texas. He is a full member and Past

President of the Texas City Management Association. He was one of the very first credentialed members of the International City/County Management Association, and served on its International Executive Board. He also served six years on the Board of Directors of the Kansas Association of City/County Management, holding all of the statewide offices including President of the Association. He is a Past President of the Kansas Engineering Society; a charter member of the Board of Directors of the Kansas Entrepreneurial Center, located at Kansas State University; and a past member of the Board of Directors of the League of Kansas Municipalities. Mr. Conduff is licensed as a Professional Engineer and a Registered Land Surveyor in the State of Kansas. He was appointed by two governors and served eight years on the Kansas State Board of Technical Professions, twice as Chairman of the Engineering Section and twice as Chairman of the Full Board.

Mike practices what he preaches while chairing and serving on a number of Boards himself. He says, "In my experience, people who give of their time and energy to serve on a Board are unbelievably caring individuals doing their absolute best to make a difference. My passion is to provide the leadership, motivation and training to give them and their professional staff the tools and insights they need to be successful."